The Banjo Player's Songbook

By Tim Jumper

Oak Publications
New York • London • Sydney

Oak Publications has conducted an exhaustive search to locate the composers, publishers, or copyright owners of the compositions in this book. However, in the event that we have inadvertently published a previously copyrighted composition without proper acknowledgement, we advise the copyright owner to contact us so that we may give appropriate credit in future editions.

Cover design by Tim Metevier
Book design by Loraine Machlin/Tim Metevier Associates
Edited by Peter Pickow

©1984 Oak Publications
A Division of Embassy Music Corporation, New York
All Rights Reserved

International Standard Book Number: 0-8256-0297-1

Exclusive Distributors:

Music Sales Corporation
257 Park Avenue South, New York, NY10010, USA

Music Sales Limited
8/9 Frith Street, London W1V 5TZ, England

Music Sales Pty. Limited
120 Rothschild Street, Rosebery, NSW 2018, Australia

Printed in Great Britain by
Redwood Books, Trowbridge, Wiltshire

To the memory of Stan Rogers (1950-1983),
singer and songwriter of Canada,
this book is respectfully dedicated.

INTRODUCTION

No other instrument is more closely identified with the spirit of American popular music than the five-string banjo. From the plunk of a skin-covered gourd in a plantation cabin, to the twang of a gold-plated Gibson on the Grand Ole Opry stage, the banjo has accompanied the songs of this land for over two hundred years.

During that time a number of different playing styles have evolved. The oldest of these, directly descended from ancient African techniques and widely popular during the middle of the nineteenth century, was known as "stroke" or "minstrel" style. With the passing of the minstrel era, the stroke style was adopted and perpetuated by musicians in the southern Appalachians, who renamed it, with characteristic verbal vigor, "frailing" or "clawhammer."

This style has much to recommend it. It is ideally suited to both vocal accompaniment and instrumental performance; it can be loud and percussive for dancing rhythms, or soft and subtle for intricate melodies; it is full-sounding enough for solo work, yet blends well with other instruments; it sounds good on any type of banjo—gut-string or steel, fretless or fretted, open-back or resonator; and, not least, it is fairly easy to learn. Thus it is not surprising that in recent years there has been a revival of interest in frailing as more and more banjo players discover and explore its possibilities.

This collection contains a wide variety of songs and tunes, most of which have never before been published for frailing or, indeed, for any style of banjo playing. These are basic arrangements within the abilities of anyone who has mastered the material covered in *How to Play Banjo*, or any banjo picker who has had about a year's experience frailing. There are no hot licks or showy displays of virtuosity in these tunes. This is simple old-time, back-porch picking for singing, dancing, and kicking out the jambs. These settings adhere closely to the melody and you should have little trouble learning unfamiliar songs right off the page. Play them as they are or use them as blueprints to guide you in constructing your own versions of the tunes.

CONTENTS

BANJO ACCOMPANIMENT: STYLES & TECHNIQUES

There are essentially two methods of instrumental accompaniment: harmonic and melodic. In harmonic accompaniment the singer simply picks or strums a rhythmic pattern on the chord changes of the song. In melodic accompaniment the singer picks the melody that is being sung, doubling it with voice and instrument. This is the method used by almost all old-time banjo players. Melodic is an outgrowth of harmonic accompaniment and can only be learned by experimentation once the more basic method has been fully assimilated.

Live performances, radio broadcasts, television appearances, recordings, and books by top-notch banjo artists are becoming increasingly available and are a rich source of ideas and inspiration for the singing banjoist. Keep your eyes and ears open.

ACCOMPANIMENT PATTERNS
IN $\frac{4}{4}$ AND $\frac{3}{4}$ TIME

The following patterns will help to stimulate your musical imagination. Experiment with them and try to come up with variations of your own. Keep in mind that all the notes ever played by your favorite picker are right there on your banjo; all you have to do is find them.

ACCOMPANIMENT PATTERNS IN $\frac{6}{8}$ TIME

$\frac{6}{8}$ time is quite common in European folk music, as in the Irish jig and the Italian tarantella. In $\frac{6}{8}$ there are six beats per measure; eighth notes receive one beat, quarter notes receive two. The first and fourth beats of the measure are stressed.

Adapting this rhythm to the banjo is a bit tricky and will require some patience to learn, because the fifth string, when it is used, is picked before the strum rather than after it.

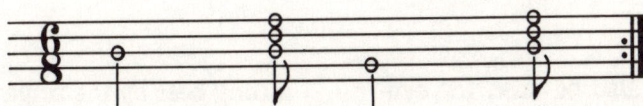

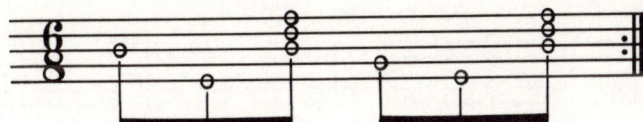

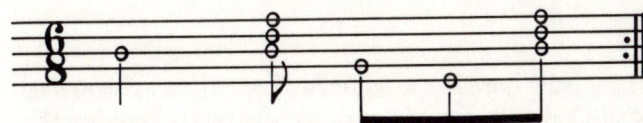

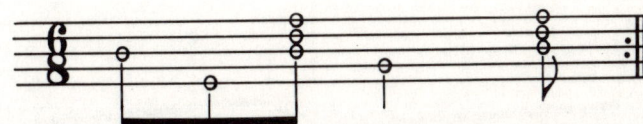

STRUMMING THE AIR

An interesting rhythmic effect can be achieved by leaving out strums while continuing to pick the fifth string on the offbeats. In order to keep the thumb's rhythm steady, the right hand makes the strumming movement in the air over the strings without hitting them, hence the term "strumming the air." This technique is useful for playing long, held notes since the notes can ring for several beats without being cut short by a strum.

The following exercise will help you get the feel of this. Omit the strums in parentheses by strumming the air. Start slowly and count out the beats carefully, then try to work up to a brisk tempo.

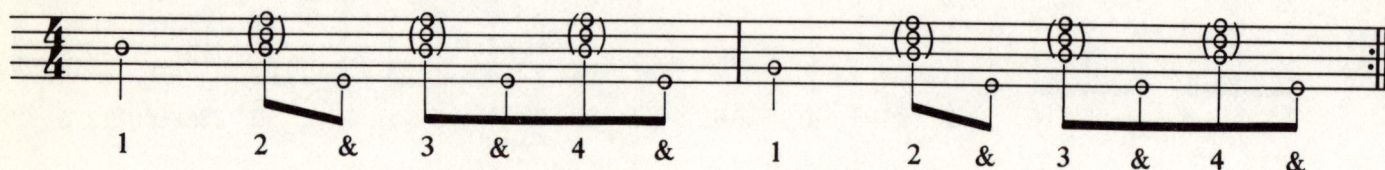

Strumming the air can also be used for syncopating rhythms by thumbing, on the weak beat, melody notes which would normally be picked on the strong beat by the finger.

Here are the first two measures of "Skip to My Lou" as usually played.

Now here is the same phrase with a syncopated beat. Omit the notes in parentheses by strumming the air.

PLECTRUM BANJO STYLE

If you were to remove the thumb-string from a five-string banjo you would have a "plectrum" banjo. This instrument, along with the tenor banjo, was popular during the 1920s. Both are still heard today in dixieland jazz bands.

You can achieve a plectrum banjo sound by resting your thumb on the fifth string to mute it while you brush down and up across the other four strings with your fingers. In the following strum patterns a single slash mark (/) stands for a down strum and is equal to one quarter-note; a double slash mark (//) stands for a down-up strum and is equal to two eighth-notes. Use any finger or fingers to strum, but be sure to keep them loose and relaxed, especially on the up strums.

This style of strumming produces a jazzier sound than the frailing strum and is useful for accompanying a variety of popular songs.

12

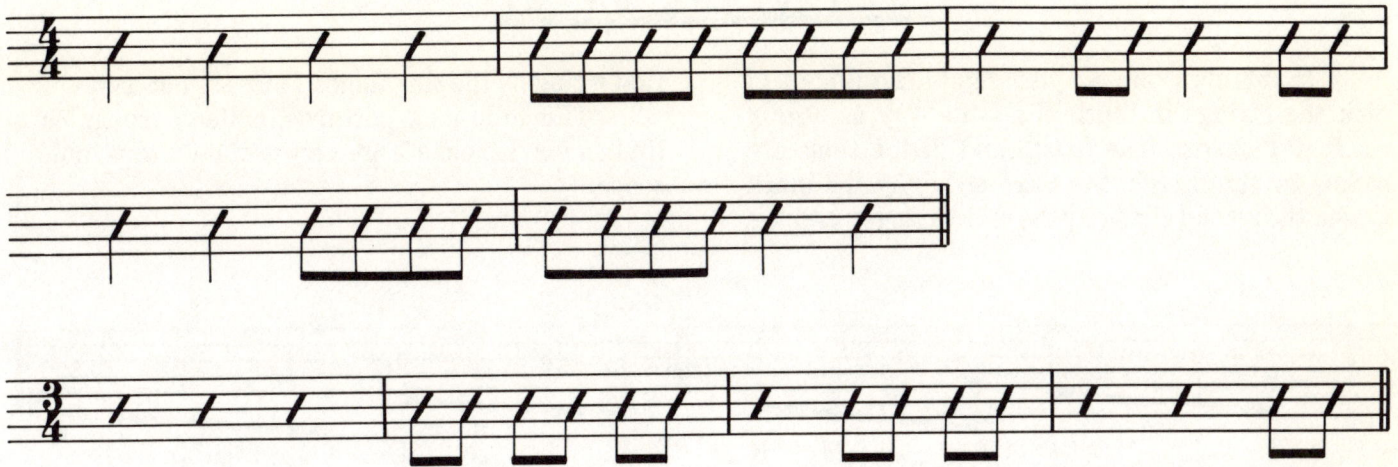

MUTING CHORDS

One way to add to a more expressive sound to the strum rhythms of the plectrum style is to mute the chords with your left hand. To do this, finger any chord in which all four strings are covered, such as C (barred fifth fret). Remember to mute the fifth string with your thumb. Brush down across the strings, then immediately relax your left-hand fingers. This will cause the sound of the chord to stop suddenly. Be careful not to lift your fingers off the strings. You should still be touching the strings, but not pressing them to the frets.

Try the following patterns and experiment to discover others.

The effect of this technique is a "chunky" sound which is well suited to many songs.

CLASSICAL STYLE

In this style you use your right-hand fingers to pick the strings in much the same way as does a classical guitarist. The fourth and fifth strings are picked by the thumb, the third string by the index finger, the second string by the middle finger, and the first string by the ring finger. Picks are not used.

The following patterns, called "arpeggios" (Italian for "harplike"), are very useful for slow, quiet songs.

THE SHUFFLE BEAT

A pair of eighth notes represents two sounds of equal length, that is, one-half beat each. In popular forms of music it is often the practice to lengthen the first note (two-thirds of a beat) and shorten the second (one-third of a beat). This alternation of long and short, called the "shuffle" beat, imparts a bounce and swing to the music, without which, according to Duke Ellington, "it don't mean a thing." Thus, any rhythm containing eighth notes can be interpreted two different ways: *straight* — eighth notes played equally (short-short) — or *shuffle* — eighth notes played unequally (long-short).

TRIPLETS

A triplet is made up of three eighth-notes which, together, equal one beat. The notes of a triplet roll are sounded by pushing the middle finger across the strings in one continuous movement, much like a slow strum. This is usually followed by a thumbed note on the fifth string.

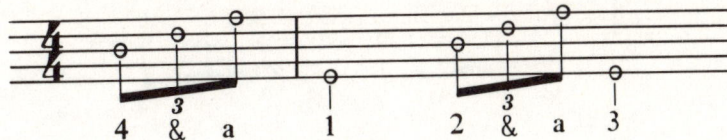

Many hornpipes begin with a triplet such as this:

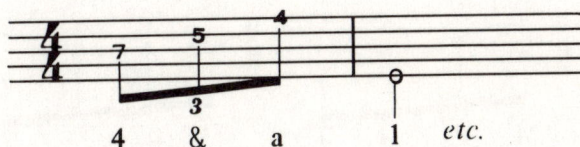

A double hammeron or a double pulloff can also be used for a triplet.

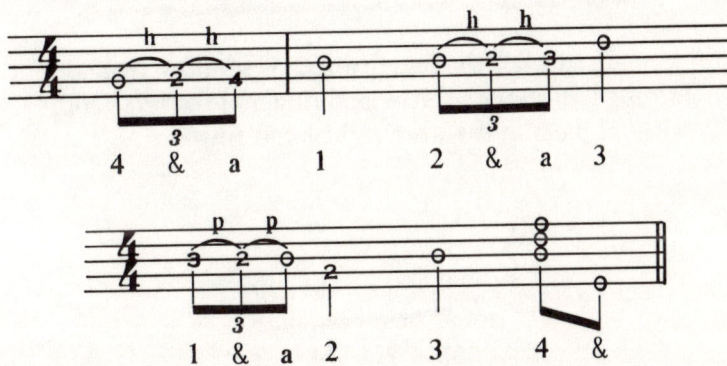

15

THE CRISP LICK

Rufus Crisp, an old-time banjo picker from Kentucky, taught this lick to Pete Seeger, who taught it to a lot of us through his book *How to Play the Five-String Banjo* (Oak Publications).

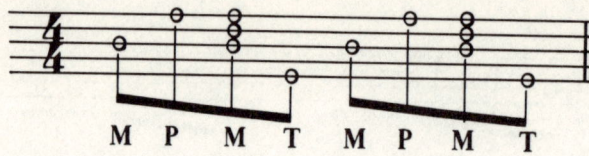

The note on the first string is sounded by picking it with a finger of the left hand. Many variations are possible:

These figures could also be played by "up-picking" the offbeat notes with the right-hand index finger.

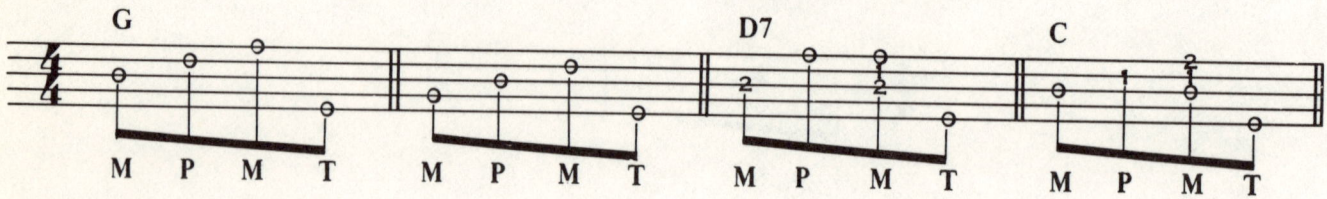

UNPICKED HAMMERONS

In this lick the fourth string is sounded by hammering it hard with the second finger of the left hand, without picking it with a right-hand finger.

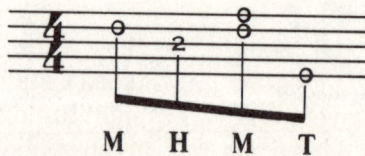

(This figure could also be played using the drop-thumb technique.)

Here are some other examples:

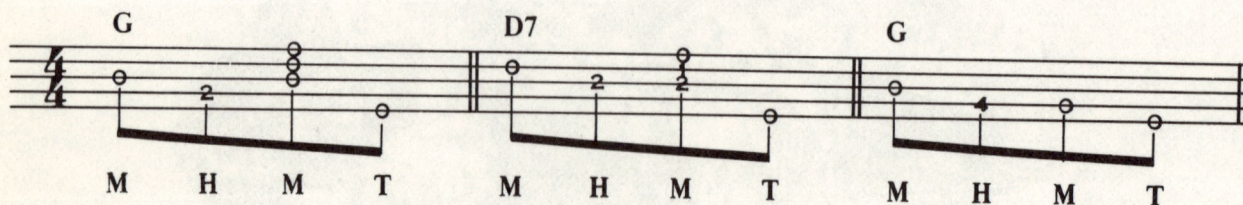

TUNINGS AND CHORDS

There are many other tunings for the banjo besides the familiar open-G. *The Folk Music Sourcebook* (Oak Publications) lists sixty-seven, and there are more that haven't been recorded. Alternate tunings allow you to perform music which would be difficult or even impossible to play in open-G, and they make possible a wide variety of unusual harmonies and interesting textures of sound. There are eight tunings used in this book. Most of the songs are in open-G (g D G B D), and that is the tuning from which the others are derived.

OPEN-G (gDGBD)

The use of this book presupposes familiarity with the open-G tuning. A detailed description of how to tune can be found on page 57 of *How to Play Banjo*, or in any good instruction book.

To tune accurately you must develop a sensitive ear, which means learning how to listen and what to listen for. A competent teacher can check to see if your banjo is properly set up, explain to you the acoustic phenomenon called "beating" (not be confused with the rhythmic concept of "beat"), explain the difference between "pitch" and "timbre," and help you with the mechanics of tuning. But in the end it comes down to this: You either hear it, or you don't. Every banjo player has had to struggle with the problems of learning to tune the instrument. It takes time. Don't get discouraged.

CHORDS IN OPEN-G TUNING

E7   E7   Em   E+5   Eadd9

E♭7   A   A7   A7   Am

Aadd9   B   B7   Bm   F

F7   F6   Fm

G-MODAL (gDGCD)

G-modal is also known as "mountain minor" or "sawmill" tuning. It produces a slightly discordant sound reminiscent of highland bagpipes, but once your ear grows accustomed to it you'll appreciate its haunting, archaic quality.

From open-G, simply raise the second string one half-tone, from B to C. The second string will sound the same as the third string, fifth fret. This tuning virtually eliminates notes on the first fret, so you can play in the second position (first finger on the second fret.)

$$\begin{array}{lll} g\ D\ G\ C\ D & & \text{G-modal} \\ & \uparrow & \\ g\ D\ G\ B\ D & & \text{open-G} \end{array}$$

CHORDS IN G-MODAL TUNING

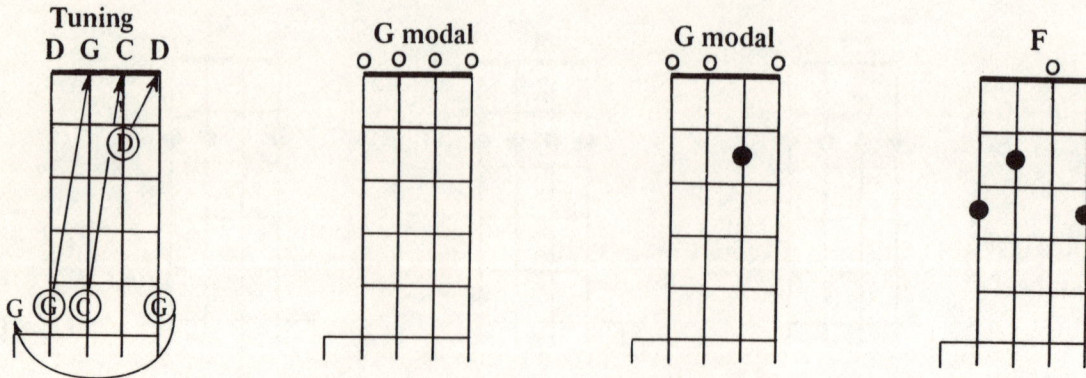

G-MINOR (gDGB♭D)

Most songs which are set in the G-modal tuning can be played in this tuning. G-minor lacks the discordant "bite" of G-modal, providing instead a rich, dark sound.

From open-G, lower the second string one half-tone, from B to B-flat. The second string will sound the same as the third string, third fret.

$$\begin{array}{lll} G\ D\ G\ B\ D & & \text{open-G} \\ & \downarrow & \\ G\ D\ G\ B♭\ D & & \text{G-minor} \end{array}$$

CHORDS IN G-MINOR TUNING

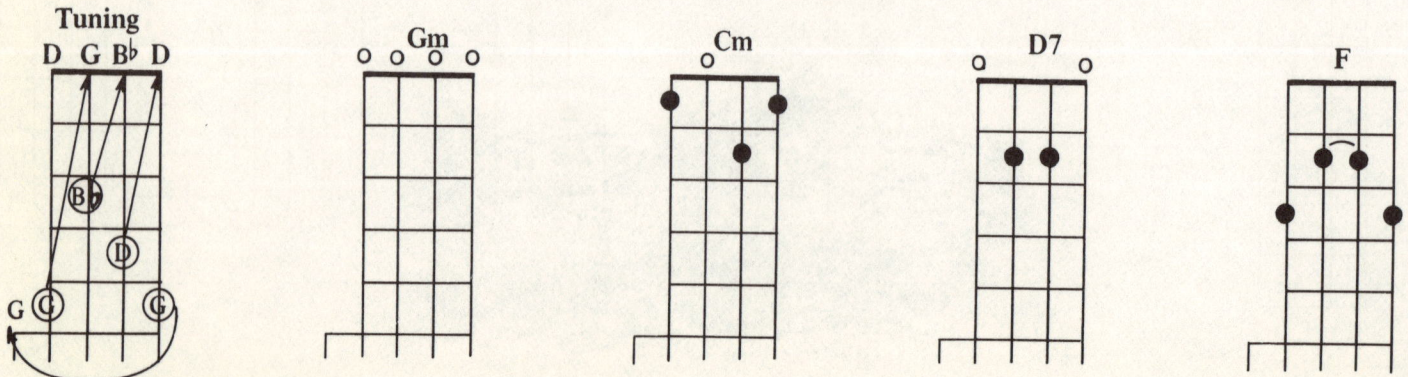

STANDARD-C (gCGBD)

This tuning is especially useful for accompanying songs in the key of C.

From open-G, lower the fourth string a whole tone, from D to C. Lowered to the correct pitch, the fourth string, seventh fret will sound the same as the open third string.

g D G B D   open-G

↓

g C G B D   standard-C

CHORDS IN STANDARD-C TUNING

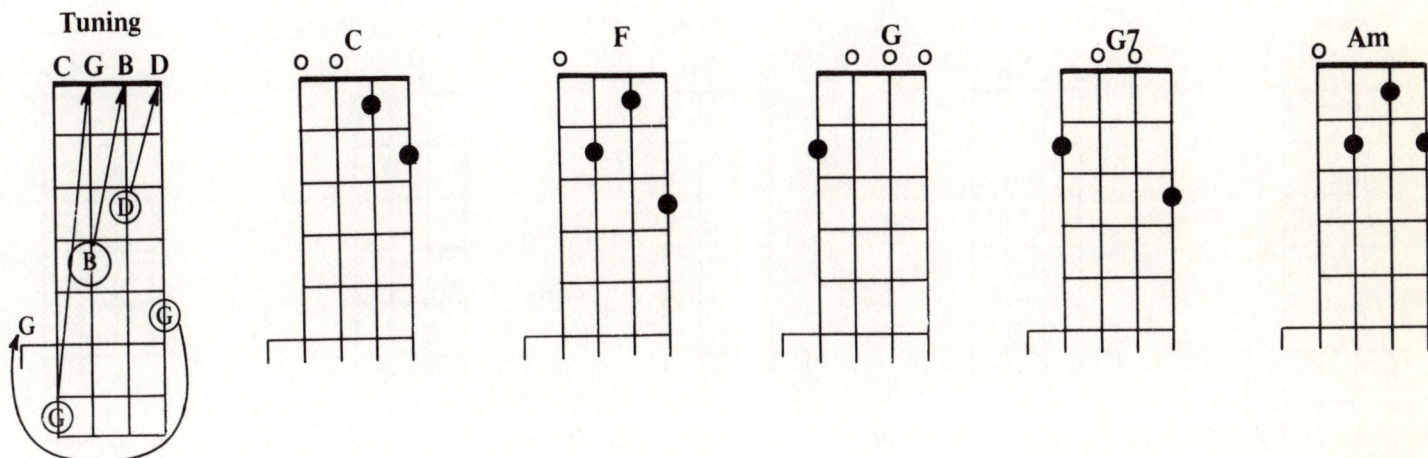

DOUBLE-C (gCGCD)

This is a very common old-time tuning and one of the most versatile.

Begin by tuning from open-G to G-modal. Then lower the fourth string one full tone, from D to C, as in the standard-C tuning. In this tuning, as in G-modal, you can play mostly in the second position.

g D G C D   G-modal

↓

g C G C D   double-C

CHORDS IN DOUBLE-C TUNING

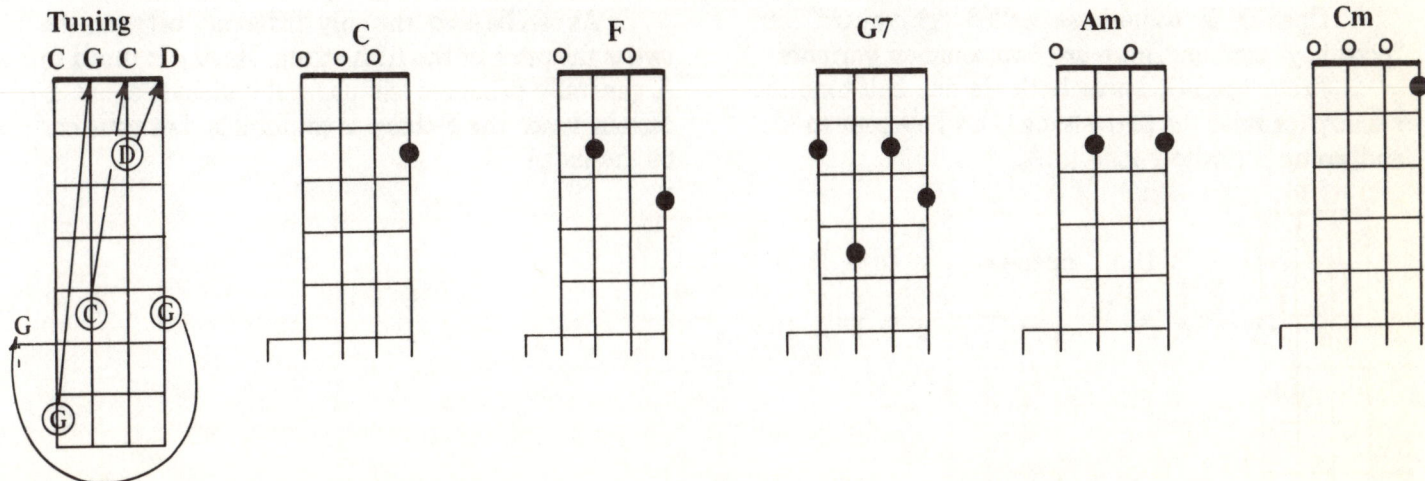

OPEN-C (gCGCE)

This was a favorite tuning of Uncle Dave Macon. It is just as easy to play in as open-G, but, being a fourth higher, produces a brighter sound.

From double-C tuning, raise the first string a whole tone, from D to E. The first string will then sound the same as the second string, fourth fret.

$$g \ C \ G \ C \ E \qquad \text{open-C}$$
$$\uparrow$$
$$g \ C \ G \ C \ D \qquad \text{double-C}$$

CHORDS IN OPEN-C TUNING

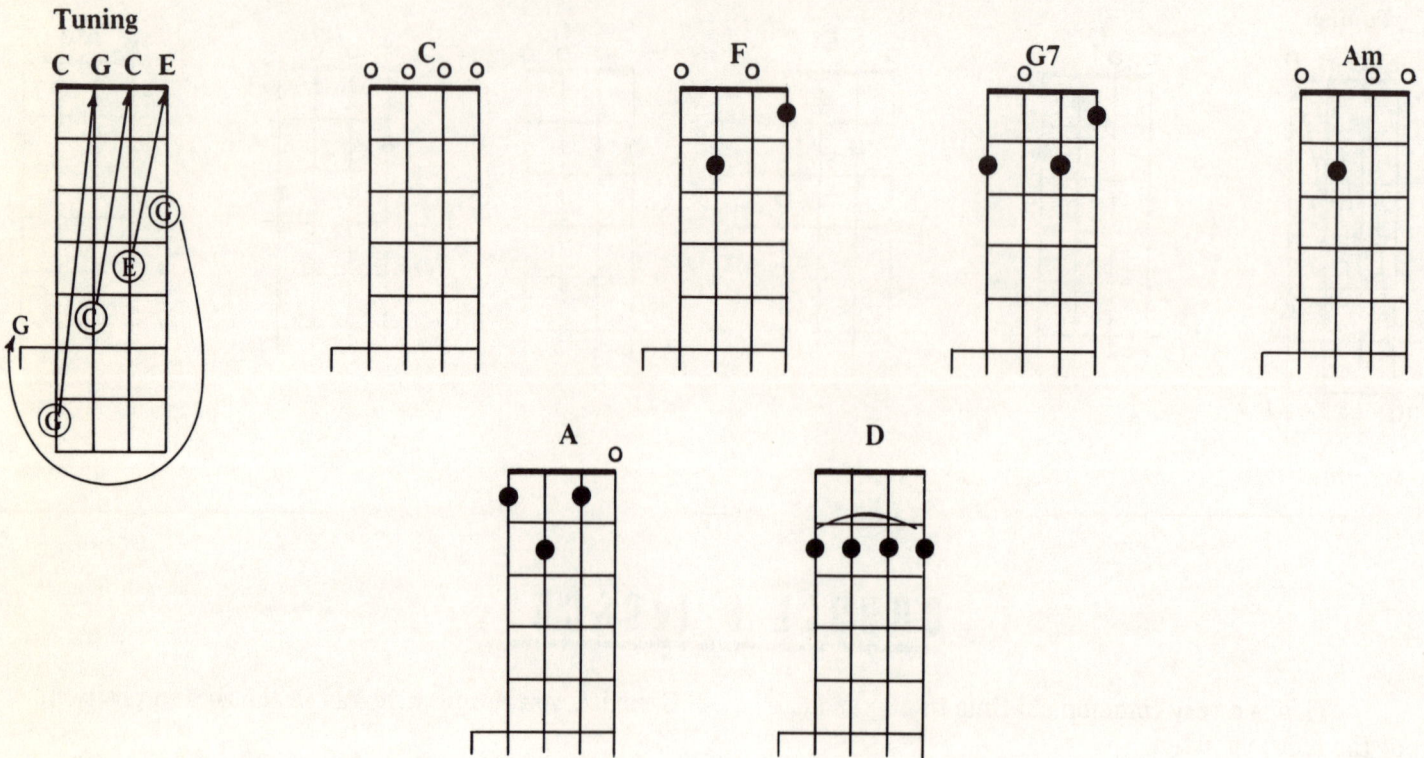

OPEN-D (aDF♯AD OR f♯DF♯AD)

Open-D is sometimes called "graveyard" or "poor boy" tuning. There are two common variants.

From open-G, lower both Gs one half-tone to F-sharp (or raise the fifth string G a whole tone to A), and lower B a whole tone to A.

As can be seen, the only difference between the two is the pitch of the fifth string. Having it tuned to A generally produces less chordal dissonance, but in certain tunes the F-sharp is preferable. Let your ear be the judge.

$$g \ D \ G \ B \ D \qquad \text{open-G}$$
$$\downarrow \ \ \downarrow \ \ \downarrow \ \downarrow$$
$$f^{\sharp} D \ F^{\sharp} A \ D \qquad \text{open-D}$$

$$\overset{a}{\underset{\uparrow}{g}} \ D \ G \ B \ D \qquad$$
$$\qquad \ \ \downarrow \ \ \downarrow$$
$$a \ D \ F^{\sharp} A \ D$$

D-MINOR (aDFAD)

This tuning produces a distinctly Oriental sound which is well suited to minor-key melodies of the Middle-East.

From open-G, tune to open-D, then lower the third string one half-tone, from F-sharp to F. The third string will sound the same as the fourth string, third fret.

a D F# A D   open-D

a D F A D   D-minor

CHORDS IN D-MINOR TUNING

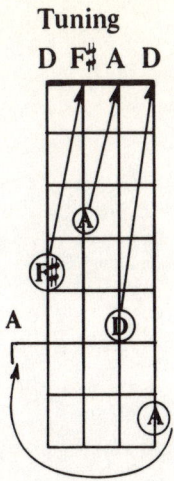

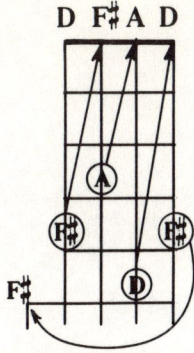

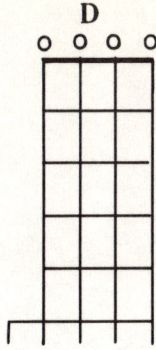

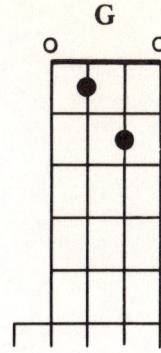

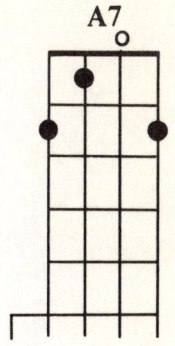

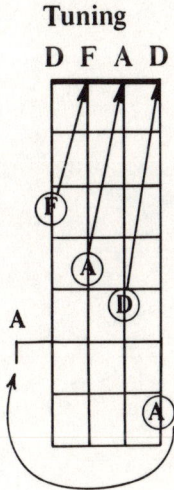

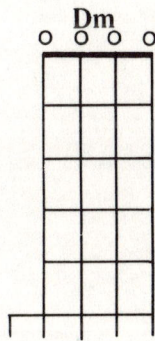

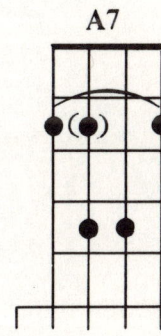

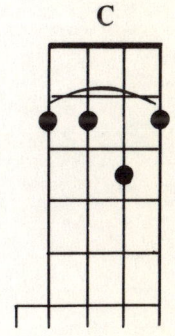

23

ALL OVER THIS LAND

CRIPPLE CREEK

This is perhaps the best knockdown banjo tune of them all. There is no better way to learn the fingerboard in open-G tuning than by working out variations on this theme.

gDGBD

Traditional

I got a gal at the head of the creek,

Goin' up to see her, 'bout the mid-dle of the week.

Kiss her on the mouth just as sweet as an-y wine,

wrap my-self a-round her like a sweet-po-ta-to vine.

Chorus:

Goin' up Crippie Creek, Goin, on the run,

Goin' up Cripple Creek, have a lit-tle fun.

Goin' up Cripple Creek, Goin' in a whirl,

Goin' up Cripple Creek. see my girl.

Cripple Creek's wide, Cripple Creek's deep,
Wade old Cripple Creek 'fore I sleep.
Hills are steep and the roads are muddy,
I'm so drunk I can't stand steady.

The gals on Cripple Creek, 'bout half grown,
Jump on a boy like a dog on a bone.
Gonna roll my britches up to my knees,
Wade old Cripple Creek when I please.

CUMBERLAND GAP

Around 1750, Dr. Thomas Walker became the first white man to explore Cumberland Gap, a gorge in the Cumberland Mountains. Twenty years later Daniel Boone led parties of settlers through the Gap into Kentucky on the trail that became known as the Wilderness Road.

Lay down boys, take a lit-tle nap,
We're all go-in' down to Cum-ber-land Gap.
Cum-ber-land Gap, Cum-ber-land Gap,
We're all go-in' down to Cum-ber-land Gap.

I got a gal in Cumberland Gap,
She's got a baby calls me pap.
    Cumberland Gap, Cumberland Gap,
We're all goin' down to Cumberland Gap.

Me and my wife, and my wife's pap,
We all live down to Cumberland Gap.
    Cumberland Gap, Cumberland Gap,
We all live down to Cumberland Gap.

DIXIE

This song, published in 1860, was the anthem of the Southern
Confederacy during the Civil War. It was written by the minstrel
entertainer Dan Emmett, a northerner, and was a favorite of Abraham
Lincoln. Play this tune for any audience of more than one person and
you're bound to get at least two Rebel yells.

gDGBD   Daniel D. Emmet

Well, I wish I was___ in the land of cot - ton,

Old times___ there are not ___ for-got-ten, Look a - way, ___ look a -

way, ___ look a - way, ___ Dix - ie Land! In ___

Dix - ie Land_ where___ I was___ born in, Ear - ly___ on one

frost - y___ morn-ing look a - way, ___ look a - way, ___ look a -

way, ___ Dix - ie Land! ___ **Chorus:** Oh, I wish I___ was in

Dix - ie, ___ Hoo - ray! ___ Hoo - ray! ___ In

Dix - ie_ Land I'll take my stand to___ live and_ die in___ Dix - ie. ___ A -

way, ___ a - way, ___ a - way down_ south in Dix - ie. A -

way, ___ a - way, ___ a - way down_ south in Dix - ie!

28

DOWN IN THE VALLEY

Over-familiarity with this tune can make you forget what a beautiful,
lonesome melody it has. Play it, sing it, and listen to it as if hearing it for
the first time.

gDGBD

Traditional

Down in the val - ley,_____ The
Hear the the wind blow,_____ dear,

val - ley so low,_____
hear the so wind blow._____

Hang your head o - ver,_____

hear the wind blow._____

Roses love sunshine, violets love dew,
Angels in heaven know I love you. *etc.*

If you don't love me, love whom you please.
Throw you arms round me, give my heart ease.

Build me a castle forty feet high
So I can see him as he rides by.

Write me a letter, send it by mail,
Send it in care of Birmingham jail.

THE ERIE CANAL

It took eight years to build this 425-mile "ditch," but when it opened in
1825 the Erie Canal became the highway to the expanding West. By 1845
there were 4,000 canal boats and 25,000 canalers afloat on the Erie, with
towpaths well worn by the hooves of as many thousand mules and horses.
These "dry-land sailors" faced some ferocious hazards, as attested to by
this song. (See also "The Cruise of the *Calibar*" for similar high adventure
on low water.)

gDGBD   Traditional

We were for - ty___ miles from Al - ban - y, for - get it I nev - er

shall,_____ What a ter - ri - ble storm we___ had that___ night on the

E - ri - e Ca - nal._____ Oh, the E - ri - e was a -

Chorus:

ris - ing_____ and the gin was a - get - ting low,_____ And I

scarce - ly ___ think we'll___ get a___ drink till we get to Buf - fa -

lo,_____ Till we get to___ Buf - fa - lo. _____

We were loaded down with barley,
We were chock full up on rye.
The captain he looked down on me
With his gol-durned wicked eye.

Two days out from Syracuse
The vessel struck a shoal.
We like to all be foundered
On a fair-sized chunk of coal.

We hollered to the captain
On the towpath treadin' dirt.
He jumped on board and stopped the leak
With his old red flannel shirt.

The cook she was a grand old gal,
She wore a ragged dress.

We heisted her upon the pole
As a signal of distress.

The winds began to whistle,
The waves began to roll.
We had to reef our royals
On that raging old canal.

When we got to Buffalo
The off-mule he was dead.
The nigh mule got blind staggers
So we cracked him on the head.

The captain he got married,
The cook she went to jail,
And I'm the only sea dog left
To tell the awful tale.

MARCHING THROUGH GEORGIA

It's too bad that such a good tune has to commemorate the most awful
and devastating campaign of the Civil War, Sherman's "March to the Sea."
Henry Clay Work portrayed it as a crusade of liberation, but in reality it
was, as General Sherman himself put it, "hell."

Henry Clay Work

gCGCE

Now bring the good old bu - gle, boys, we'll sing an - oth - er song, Sing it with a spir - it that will start the world a - long. Oh, sing it as we used to sing it, fif - ty thou - sand strong, While we were march - ing through Geor - gia. Hur - rah, hur - rah, we bring the ju - bi - lee. Hur - rah, hur - rah, the flag that makes you free! And so we sang the cho - rus from At - lan - ta to the sea While we were march - ing through Geor - gia.

31

HOME ON THE RANGE

Folklorists have determined that this song has been around since at least the 1860s. Its ultimate origins have proved impossible to trace. Whoever wrote it certainly captured the spirit of the American West in its most romantic aspect.

gDGBD

Anonymous

Oh, give me a home where the buf - fa - lo roam, Where the

deer and the an - te - lope play; Where

sel - dom is heard a dis - cour - a - ging word, And the

skies are not cloud - y all day.

Chorus:

Home, home on the range, Where the

deer and the an - te - lope play; Where

sel - dom is heard a dis - cour - a - ging word And the

skies are not cloud - y all day.

How often at night when the heavens are bright
With the lights from the glittering stars;
Have I stood there amazed and asked as I gazed
If their glory exceeds that of ours.

Oh, give me a land where the bright diamond sand
Flows leisurely down the stream;
Where the graceful white swan goes gliding along
Like a maid in a heavenly dream.

Where the air is so pure, the zephyrs so free,
The breezes so balmy and light,
That I would not exchange my home on the range
For all of the cities so bright.

Oh, I love those white flowers in this dear land of ours,
The curlew I love to hear scream,
And I love the white rocks and the antelope flocks
That graze on the mountaintops green.

ON TOP OF OLD SMOKY

The roots of this mountain ballad can be traced back to the British Isles,
the source of so much of our traditional music. This is, of course, the air
used in the beloved schoolyard classic, "On top of Spaghetti."

On___ top of Old Smok - y,___
Now___ court - ing is pleas - ure___

all cov - ered with snow,___
and part - ing is grief,___

I___ lost my true
But a false - heart - ed

lov - er,___ for___
lov - er is ___

court - ing too slow.___
worse than a thief.___

A thief will just rob you and take what you have,
But a falsehearted lover will lead you to the grave.
And the grave will decay you and turn you to dust;
Not one boy in a hundred a poor girl can trust.

They'll hug you and kiss you and tell you more lies
Than the cross-ties on the railroad or the stars in the skies.
So come all you young maidens and listen to me,
Never place your affection on a green willow tree.

For the leaves they will wither and the roots they will die;
You'll all be forsaken and never know why.
On top of Old Smoky all covered with snow,
I lost my true lover for courting too slow.

SACRAMENTO

A sea chantey from the gold-rush days which combines elements of Jesse
Hutchinson's "Ho! For California!" and Stephen Foster's "Camptown
Races," along with the usual chanteyman's couplets. Roar it out!

gDGBD

Traditional

A ___ bul - ly ship and a bul - ly ___ crew, To me
hoo - dah, ___ to me hoo - dah, ___ A ___ bul - ly ___ mate and a
cap - tain ___ too, To me hoo - dah, ___ hoo - dah ___ day. ___ Then
blow, ___ boys, ___ blow, ___ For Cal - i - for - ni -
o. ___ There's plen - ty of ___ gold, ___ so ___ I've been told, On the
banks of the Sac - ra - men - to.

Round Cape Horn in the month of snows, *etc.*
If we get there nobody knows,

To the Sacramento we're bound away,
To the Sacramento's a hell of a way.

Ninety days to Frisco Bay,
Ninety days is damn good pay.

When you're beating round Cape Horn,
You'll wish to God you'd never been born.

34

SOURWOOD MOUNTAIN

Art Rosenbaum in *Old-Time Mountain Banjo* quotes Professor Josiah
Coombs describing a mountain minstrel in the words of a judge to a jury:
*Gentlemen: Whenever you see a great big overgrown buck sitting at the
mouth of some holler, or at the forks of some road, with a big slouch hat
on, a blue celluloid collar, a celluloid artificial red rose in his coat lapel, a
banjo strung across his breast, and a-pickin' of "Sourwood Mountain," fine
that man, gentlemen, fine him! For if he hasn't already done something,
he's a-goin' to.*

Traditional

gDGBD

Chick - ens__ crow - in' on__ Sour - wood__ Moun - tain,

Hey,_____ ho,_____ did - dle - um day.____

So man - y pret - ty girls,___ I___ can't___ count 'em,

Hey,_____ ho,_____ did - dle - um day.____

My true love's a blue-eyed daisy, *etc.*
If I don't get her I'll go crazy,

My love lives at the head of the holler,
She won't come and I won't foller,

My love lives just over the river,
Few more jumps and I'll be with her,

Ducks in the pond, geese in the ocean,
Devil's in the women when they take a notion,

SUGAR HILL

This song courtesy of the Sugar Hill Chamber of Commerce.

Lyrics under the staff:

If you want to get your eye knocked out, If you want to get your fill, If you want to get your eye knocked out, Go to Sugar Hill.

RAISE A RUCKUS

AIN'T GONNA WORK TOMORROW

Some folks will use any excuse to get a day off.

gDGBD

Traditional

I ain't _____ gon - na _____ work _____ to -
mor - row, _____ Ain't _____ gon - na _____
work _____ to - day, _____
Ain't _____ gon - na _____ work _____ to - mor - row,
Lord, _____ For _____ that _____ is my wed - ding _____
day. _____

I've been all around this country,
Been all around this world,
Been all around this country, Lord,
For the sake of one little girl.

I love my dear old mama,
Love my papa, too,
Love my dear old mama, Lord,
But I'd leave 'em just to go with you.

I'm just a lonesome traveler,
Singing my lonesome song,
I'm just a lonesome traveler, Lord,
I'll be gone 'fore long.

38

SHE'LL BE COMIN' ROUND THE MOUNTAIN

Samuel Beckett meets Gertrude Stein.

gDGBD

Traditional

She'll be com - in' round the moun - tain when she comes, She'll be com - in' round the moun - tain when she comes, She'll be com - in' round the mountain. She'll be com - in' round the mountain, She'll be com - in' round the moun - tain when she comes.

She'll be drivin' six white horses when she comes, *etc.*

We'll all go out to meet her when she comes,

We'll kill the old red rooster when she comes,

We'll all have chicken and dumplins when she comes,

BIG BALL'S IN TOWN

Feel free to insert the town of your choice in the appropriate measures.

gDGBD

Traditional

Chorus:

(banjo tablature)

Big ball's _____ in Bos - ton, _____

big ball's _____ in town, _____

Big ball's _____ in Bos - ton, _____

we'll dance _____ a round. _____

Work on the railroad, sleep on the ground,
Eat sody crackers, ten cents a pound.

Get on your big shoes, get on your gown
Shake off those sad blues, big ball's in town.

Let's have a party, let's have a time,
Let's have a party, I've got a dime.

I'll stay in Boston, I'll stick around,
I'll stay in Boston, big ball's in town.

Get drunk in Boston, dance round the town,
Board up your windows, big ball's in town.

HOT CORN, COLD CORN

Corn "likker" (a.k.a. "white lightning") has long been the mainstay of
mountain conviviality.

gDGBD

Traditional

Chorus:

(banjo tablature)

Hot corn, _____ cold corn, _____ bring a - long a dem - i - john, _____

Hot corn, _____ cold corn, _____ bring a - long a dem - i - john, _____

Hot corn, _____ cold corn, _____ bring a - long a dem - i - john, _____

Fare thee well,___ Un-cle Bill,___ see you in the morn-ing,___

Yes,___ sir.

Upstairs, downstairs, out in the kitchen, *(three times)*
Met an old cook just a-reeling and a-pitching,
Yes sir.

Preacher is a-hollering, children are a-crying,
Chicken heads a-wringing and toenails a-flying,
Yes sir.

Old Aunt Sally, won't you fill 'em up again,
I ain't had a drink since Lord knows when,
Yes sir.

JUBILEE

This is one of those tunes that's such fun to pick and sing that you'll want
to make up more verses just to keep it going.

gDGBD

Traditional

All out___ on the___ old rail - road,___ all out___ on the

sea,___ All out___ on___ the___ old rail - road,___

Far as I can see.___ Swing and turn,___ ju - bi -

lee;___ live and learn,___ ju - bi - lee,___ Swing and___

turn,___ ju - bi - lee,___ live and learn,___ ju - bi - lee.___

Hardest work I ever done, workin' on the farm;
Easiest work I ever done, in my truelove's arms.

I won't have no widder man, neither will my cousin;
You can get them widder men fifteen cents a dozen.

If I had a needle and thread, fine as I could sew,
I'd sew my truelove to my side and down the road I'd go.

WATERBOUND

A flash flood in the mountains could wipe out a bridge and leave an
ardent lover fortunately stranded with his girl at her father's cabin. These
days a young swain achieves similar results by running out of gas on
Lovers' Lane.

gDGBD
Traditional

Wa - ter - bound__ and I can't get home,_____

Wa - ter - bound and I can't__ get home,_____

Wa - ter - bound__ and I can't get home, Way__

down__ in North__ Car - o - lin - a.

Chickens crowin' in the old plowed field *(three times)*
  Down in North Carolina.

Nick and Charlie left to go home
  Before the water rises.

The old man's mad but I don't care,
  I'm going to marry his daughter.

If he don't give her up we're gonna run away
  Down in North Carolina.

42

KEEP MY SKILLET GOOD AND GREASY

To appreciate the full flavor of the line, pronounce it "greazy." Endeavor
to eschew urbanized accentual refinement in this composition.

gDGBD　　　　　　　　　　　　　　　　　　　　　　　　　　**Traditional**

Gon - na　buy＿ me a sack＿ of ＿ flour; ＿ bake me ＿
hoe - cake ＿ ev - ery hour, ＿ Keep my ＿
skil - let ＿ good and greas - y ＿ all the
time, ＿ time, ＿ time, ＿ Keep my ＿
skil - let ＿ good and greas - y ＿ all the
time. ＿

Honey, if you say so, I'll never work no more,
I'll lay around your shanty all the time, time, time,
Lay around your shanty all the time.

Got some chickens in the sack; got the bloodhounds on my track.
Keep my skillet good and greasy all the time, time, time,
Keep my skillet good and greasy all the time.

Gonna buy me a jug of brandy; gonna give it all to Mandy;
Keep her good and drunk and boozy all the time, time, time,
Good and drunk and boozy all the time.

SHORT'NIN' BREAD

A great song for bouncing a baby on your knee. Just remember to remove
your banjo first.

Traditional

Two___ lit - tle chil - dren___ ly - in' in___ bed,___

One___ was___ sick___ and the oth - er 'most___ dead.___

Sent___ for the doc - tor and the doc - tor___ said,___

"Feed___ them___ chil - dren some short' - nin'___ bread."

Chorus: G

Mam - my's lit - tle ba - by loves___ short' - nin',___ short' - nin',___

Mam - my's lit - tle ba - by loves___ short' - nin'___ bread.___

Put on the skillet, put on the lid,
Mammy's gonna make a little short'nin' bread.
That ain't all she's gonna do,
Mammy's gonna make a little coffee, too.

Go in the kitchen, lift up the lid,
Fill my pockets with short'nin' bread.
Stole the skillet, stole the lid,
Stole the gal making short'nin' bread.

Caught with the skillet, caught with the lid,
Caught with the gal making short'nin' bread.
A dollar for the skillet, a dollar for the lid,
A month in jail for eatin' short'nin' bread.

WAY DOWN THE OLD PLANK ROAD

This song comes down to us from the greatest banjo entertainer of them
all, Uncle Dave Macon. To quote Art Rosenbaum again: *The learning
banjo picker may feel a little reticent about twirling his instrument
through the air in the middle of a song, or yelling "Hot Dog!" or "Glory,
Hallelujah Damn!" during a break. But certainly you should listen to a lot
of Uncle Dave's records and try to feel in your own voice and fingers
some of the joyous drive and syncopation of this music.*

gDGBD

Traditional

Rath - er be in Rich - mond with

all the hail and rain,

Than for to be in Geor - gia, boys,

wear-ing that ball and chain.

Chorus:

Won't get drunk no more,

won't get drunk no more,

Won't get drunk no more, way

down the old plank road.

I went down to Mobile but I get on the gravel train,
Very next thing they heard of me, had on the ball and chain.

Doney, oh dear Doney, what makes you treat me so?
Caused me to wear the ball and chain, now my ankle's sore.

Knoxville is a pretty place, Memphis is a beauty,
Want to see them pretty gals, hop to Chattanoogie.

BILE 'EM CABBAGE DOWN

"Biled" cabbage smells pretty awful but it sounds great on the banjo. For
many of us this was the first song we learned to pick.

gDGBD

Traditional

Went up on the mountain just to give my horn a blow,

Thought I heard my true-love say,

"Yonder comes my beau."

Chorus:

Bile 'em cabbage down, down; bake 'em hoe-cakes brown,

Only song that I can sing is bile 'em cabbage down.

Possum up a 'simmon tree, raccoon on the ground,
Raccoon says, "You son-of-a-gun, shake some 'simmons down."

Someone stole my old coon dog, wish they'd bring him back,
He chased the big hogs through the fence and the little ones through the crack.

Met a possum on the road, blind as he could be,
Jumped the fence and whupped my dog and bristled up at me.

Once I had an old gray mule, name was Simon Slick,
He'd roll his eyes and back his ears and how that mule would kick.

How that mule would kick, he kicked with his dying breath,
He shoved his hind feet down his throat and kicked himself to death!

WILD ROVERS

THE BLACK VELVET BAND

Van Dieman's Land, now called Tasmania, was the site of a British penal colony.

gDGBD   Traditional

In a neat lit - tle___ town they call Bel -

fast,___ Ap - pren - tice to trade I was bound.___

And___ man - y an___ hour of sweet hap - pi -

ness___ Have I spent in that neat lit - tle town.___

But a sad___ mis - for - tune came o - ver___

me___ That caused me to___ stray from the land,___

Far a - way from___ my___ friends and re - la -

tions,___ Be - trayed by the black vel - vet band.___

Chorus:

Her eyes___ they___ shone like the dia -

monds, ___ You'd think she was queen of the land.___

48

And her hair___ hung___ o - ver her shoul -

der___ Tied___ up with a___ black vel - vet band.___

I took a stroll down Broadway,
Not meaning to stray very far,
When who should I meet but a pretty fair maid
Peddling her trade in a bar.
She stole a gold watch from a gentleman
And placed it right into my hand.
And the very first thing that I thought was,
"Bad 'cess to the black velvet band."

Before the judge and the jury
I soon was forced to appear.
The judge he says to me, "Me lad,
Your case it is sad but clear.
I'll give you ten years penal servitude
To be spent far away from the land,
Far away from your friends and relations,
Betrayed by the black velvet band."

Come all you jolly young fellows,
A warning take by me.
When you are out on the town, me lads,
Beware of the pretty colleens.
They'll fill you with strong drink, me lads,
Till you are unable to stand.
And the very next thing that you notice is
You've landed in Van Dieman's Land.

THE WILD ROVER

Methinks this rover doth protest too much.

gDGBD

Traditional

I've___ been a wild rov - er for___ man - y a year.___ And I've spent all my___ mon - ey on whis - key and beer.___ But___ now I'm re - turn - ing with___ gold in great store.___ And I swear I will___ play the wild rov - er no more. And it's no,___ nay,___ nev - er,___ No, nay,___ nev - er no more,___ Will I play___ the wild rov - er,___ No, nev - er no more.___

I went into an alehouse I used to frequent
And I told the landlady my money was spent.
I asked her for credit, she answered me, "Nay,
Such custom as yours I can get any day."

Put my hand in my pocket, took out sovereigns bright,
And the landlady's eyes opened wide with delight.
She said, "I have whiskey and wine of the best.
The words that I spoke, sir, were only in jest."

Going back to my parents, confess what I've done,
And beg them to pardon their prodigal son.
And if they forgive me, as ofttimes before,
I swear I will play the wild rover no more.

TO THE BEGGING I WILL GO

When you have enough to live on, you have enough.

gDGBD

Traditional

Of all the trades that ev - er was the beg - ging is the best, For when a beg - gar's tired he can lay him down to rest. To the beg - ging I will go, go, To the beg - ging I will go.

I've a pocket for my oatmeal and another for my salt.
I've a pair of little crutches, you should see how I can halt.

There's patches on my dusty coat, another for my ee',
But when it comes to pints of ale I can see as well as thee.

My britches they are nought but holes, but my heart is free from care;
As long as I've my belly full, my backside can go bare.

I can rest my head where'er I choose and I don't pay no rent.
I've got no noisy loons to mind and I am right content.

I can rest when I am tired and I heed no master's bell.
A man is daft to be a king when a beggar lives so well.

THE WILD COLONIAL BOY

Australia has had its share of rough-and-ready heroes. Jack Duggan was a
sort of down-under Robin Hood.

gDGBD **Traditional**

It's of _____ a wild _____ co - lo - nial _____ boy, _____ Jack _____ Dug - gan _____ was _____ his _____ name. _____ He was born _____ and raised _____ in Ire - land, in a place _____ called _____ Cas - tle - main, _____ Well, he was _____ his fa - ther's on - ly _____ son, _____ his moth - er's _____ pride _____ and _____ joy. _____ And dear - ly _____ did _____ his par - ents _____ love _____ the wild _____ co - lo - nial _____ boy. _____

52

At the early age of sixteen years he left his native home
And to Australia's sunny clime he was inclined to roam.
He robbed the rich to help the poor, he shot James McEvoy.
A terror to Australia was the wild colonial boy.

One morning on the prairie, as Jackie rode along,
Listening to the mockingbird singing a cheerful song,
Up stepped a band of troopers, Kelly, Davis, and Fitzroy.
They all set out to capture him, the wild colonial boy.

"Surrender now, Jack Duggan, for you see we're three to one.
Surrender in the king's high name, for you're a plundering son."
Jack drew two pistols from his belt and proudly raised them high.
"I'll fight but not surrender," said the wild colonial boy.

He fired a shot at Kelly which struck him to the ground,
Then turning round to Davis he received a fatal wound.
The bullet pierced his proud young heart from the pistol of Fitzroy,
And that was how they captured him, the wild colonial boy.

WHISKEY IN THE JAR

This tune is also known as "Kilgarry Mountain."

I counted out his money and it made a pretty penny,
I put it in my pocket and I took it home to Jenny.
She sighed and she swore that she never would deceive me,
But the devil take the women for they never can be easy..

I went up to my chamber all for to take a slumber,
I dreamt of gold and jewels and for sure it was no wonder.
But Jenny drew my charges and she filled them up with water,
Then sent for Captain Farrell to be ready for the slaughter.

'Twas early the next morning when I arose to travel,
Up stepped a band of footmen and likewise Captain Farrell.
I drew forth my pistol for she'd stolen away my rapier,
But I couldn't shoot the water so a prisoner I was taken.

Now if anyone can aid me 'tis my brother in the army,
If I can find his station in Cork or in Killarney.
And if he'll go with me, we'll go rolling through Killkenny,
And sure he'll treat me better than my own missporting Jenny.

Now there's some take delight in the carriages a-rolling,
And others take delight in the hurley and the bowling.
But I take delight in the juice of the barley
And courting pretty fair maids in the morning bright and early.

ROVING GAMBLER

The riverboat gambler is one of the classic characters of frontier
mythology. The ladies, supposedly, found him irresistibly attractive.

gDGBD   Traditional

I am a roving gambler, I've
gambled all around, And when-ev-er I meet with a
deck of cards I lay my mon-ey down,
Lay my mon-ey down, Lord, lay my mon-ey
down.

I've gambled down in Washington,
I've gambled up in Maine.
I'm on my way to Georgia, boys,
To knock down my last game,
    Knock down my last game, Lord, knock down my last game.

I wasn't down in Washington
Many more weeks than three,
I fell in love with a pretty little gal,
She fell in love with me, *etc.*

She took me to her parlor,
Cooled me with her fan.

She whispered to her mother,
"I love this gambling man,

"Wouldn't marry a railroad man,
This is the reason why:
I never saw a railroad man
Wouldn't tell his wife a lie,

"Oh mother dear, oh mother,
I'll tell you if I can.
If you ever see me coming back,
It'll be with a gambling man,

55

BUNGLE RYE

Another cautionary tale of a good-natured sailor and a scheming damsel.

gDGBD   G   **Traditional**

Well, Jack was a sail - or who walked through Ross - town, And she was a dam - sel who skipped up and down. Said the dam - sel to Jack, as she passed him by, "Would you care for to purchase some queer bun - gle rye, rad - dy - rye?" Fol - the - did - dle - aye, rad - dy - rye, rad - dy - rye.

Says Jack to himself, "Now what could it be,
But the finest old whiskey from far Germany,
Smuggled up in a basket and sold on the sly,
And the name that it goes by is queer bungle rye, raddy-rye."
    Fol-the-diddle-aye, raddy-rye, raddy-rye.

Jack gave her a pound, for he thought nothing strange.
"Hold the basket, young man, while I run for your change."
Jack looked in the basket and a kid he did spy,
"I'll be damned, then," says Jack, "This is queer bungle rye, raddy-rye."
    Fol-the-diddle-aye, raddy-rye, raddy-rye.

To get the child christened was Jack's first intent,
To get the child christened to the parson he went.
Says the parson to Jack, "What will he go by?"
"I'll be damned, then," says Jack, "Call him queer bungle rye, raddy-rye."
    Fol-the-diddle-aye, raddy-rye, raddy-rye.

Says the parson to Jack, "That's a very queer name."
"I'll be damned, then," says Jack, "And a queer way he came.
All wrapped in a basket and sold on the sly,
And the name that he goes by is queer bungle rye, raddy-rye."
    Fol-the-diddle-aye, raddy-rye, raddy-rye.

Now all you young sailors who walk through the town,
Beware of the damsels who skip up and down.
Take a look in their baskets as they pass you by,
Or else they may pawn on you queer bungle rye, raddy-rye.
    Fol-the-diddle-aye, raddy-rye, raddy-rye.

I'M A ROVER

This Scottish tune has one of the best of all singalong choruses. Gather a
crowd and belt it out!

gDGBD   **Traditional**

Though the___ night___ be___ dark___ as___ dun -

geon,___ No' a star___ to be___ seen a -

bove,___ I___ will be guid -

ded with - out___ a___ stum - ble___ To___ the___

airms___ o' my___ ain true - love.

Chorus:

I'm a rov - er, sel - dom

so - ber. I'm a rov - er o' high de -

gree, It's___ when___ I'm___ drink -

ing I'm___ al - ways___ think - ing___ How___ to___

gain___ my___ love's___ com - pa - ny.

He steppit up to her bedroom window,   She raised her head on her snow-white pillow,
Kneelin' gently upon a stone.   Wi' her airms aboot her breast,
He rappit at her bedroom window,   "Who is that at my bedroom window,
"Darlin' dear, do you lie alone?"   Disturbin' me at my lang nicht's rest?"

"It's only me, your ain true-lover.
Open the door and let me in
For I hae come on a lang, lang journey,
And I'm near drenched to the skin."

She opened the door wi' the greatest pleasure,
She opened the door and she let him in.
They baith shook hands and embraced each other;
Till the morning they lay as one.

The cocks were crawin', the birds were whistlin';
The burns they ran free abune the brae,
"Remember, lass, I'm a ploughman laddie
And the fairmer I must obey.

"Noo, my lass, I maun gang and leave thee.
Though the hills they be high above,
I will climb them wi' greater pleasure
Since I been in the airms o' my love."

GYPSY DAVY

This is a somewhat Americanized version of an old English ballad.

gDGBD   **Traditional**

It was late last___ night when the boss came home,___

Ask - in'___ for his___ la - dy.___ The

on - ly___ an - swer___ that he got: "She's___

gone with the Gyp - sy Dav - y, She's___

gone with the Gyp - sy Dave."___

"Go saddle me my buckskin horse,
My hundred dollar saddle.
Point out to me their wagon tracks
And after them I'll travel,
After them I'll ride."

He had not rode to the midnight moon
When he saw their campfire gleaming.
He heard the notes of a big guitar
And the voice of the gypsy singing,
The song of the Gypsy Dave.

"Take off, take off your kidskin gloves,
Your boots of Spanish leather,
And give to me your lily-white hands,
We'll go home together,
Back home again we'll ride."

"No, I won't take off my kidskin gloves,
My boots of Spanish leather.
I'll go my way from day to day
And sing with the Gypsy Davy,
The song of the Gypsy Dave."

"Have you forsaken your house and home?
Have you forsaken your baby?
Have you forsaken your husband dear
To go with the Gypsy Davy,
And sing with the Gypsy Dave?"

"Yes, I've forsaken my house and home
To go with the Gypsy Davy.
And I've forsaken my husband dear
But not my blue-eyed baby,
My pretty blue-eyed babe."

THE CALTON WEAVER

There's something to be said for the quiet life of weaving after all.

gDGBD

Traditional

I _____ am a weav - er, a Cal - ton _____

weav - er. _____ I _____ am a rash _____ and a

rov - ing _____ blade. I've _____ got _____

sil - ver _____ in _____ my _____ for - tune, _____

I'll _____ go and for - low the rov - ing _____

Chorus:

trade. _____ Whis - ky, Whis - ky, _____

Nan - cy _____ Whis - ky, _____ Whis - ky,

Whis - ky, _____ Nan - cy - o!

60

As I came in by Glasgow city,
Nancy Whisky I chanced to smell.
I went in, sat down beside her,
Seven long years and I've loved her well.

The more I kissed her, the more I loved her.
The more I kissed her, the more she smiled,
Till I forgot my mother's teaching,
Nancy Whisky had me beguiled.

I awoke early in the morning,
To wet my thirst it was my need.
I tried to rise but I was not able,
Nancy Whisky had me by the head.

"Come, landlady, what's the lawing?
Tell me what there is to pay."
"Fifteen shillings is the reckoning.
Pay me quickly and go away."

I'll go back to the Calton weaving,
I'll surely make the shuttles fly,
For I'll make more at the Calton weaving,
Than ever I did in the roving way.

Come all ye weavers, ye Calton weavers,
Come all ye weavers where'er ye be,
Beware of Whisky, Nancy Whisky,
She'll ruin you as she's ruined me.

HI FOR THE BEGGARMAN

Beggars, as well as frogs, often turn out to be princes. Some would say
that's taking a step or two down.

gDGBD

Oh, the night be - ing dark and ver - y cold, A
wom - an took pit - y on a poor old soul.
She took pit - y on a poor old soul And she asked him to come
in. Chorus: With me too - roo - roo - roo rant - in' hi, With me
too - roo - roo - roo rant - in' hi, Too - roo - roo - roo
rant - in' hi, And hi for the beg - gar - man.

He sat him down in the chimney nook,
He hung his coat upon a hook,
He hung his coat upon a hook
And merrily he did sing.

In the middle of the night the old one rose,
She missed the beggarman and all his clothes.
She clapped and clapped and clapped again,
Saying, "He's with me daughter gone."

Three long years have passed and gone
When this old man came back again
Asking for some charity,
"Would you lodge a beggarman?"

"I never lodged any but the one
And with that one me daughter's gone,
With that one me daughter's gone
So merrily ye may go."

"Would you like to see your daughter now,
With two babies on her knee,
With two babies on her knee,
And another one coming on?

"For yonder she sits and yonder she stands,
The finest lady in all the land
Servants all at her command,
Since she went with the beggarman."

FILL THE FLOWING BOWL: DRINKING SONGS

MOUNTAIN TAY

Tea is pronounced *tay* in Ireland. Such illegal whiskey, also called 'poteen',
has been distilled in the remote hills by generations of thirsty Irishmen.

Chorus:

gDGBD

S. McCarthy

Gath - er up the pots and the old tin can, The
mash, the corn, the bar - ley, and the bran,
Run like the de - vil from the ex - cise - man, Keep the
smoke from ris - ing, Bar - ney.
Keep your eyes well peeled to - day, The
big tall men are on their way,
Search - ing for the moun - tain tay In the
hills of Con - ne ma - ra.

There's a gallon for the butcher, a quart for Tom,
A bottle for poor old Father John,
To help his prayers and hymns along
   In the hills of Connemara.

Stand your ground, boys, it's too late,
The excisemen are at the gate.
Glory be to God the drinkin' is neat
   In the hills of Connemara.

Swing to the left and swing to the right,
The excisemen will dance all night,
Drinkin' up the tay till the broad daylight
   In the hills of Connemara.

THE JUG OF PUNCH

In which are extolled the amazing medicinal properties of Irish punch.

gDGBD

Traditional

As I was sit - ting_____ with me jug and spoon,_____ One_____ pleas - ant_____ even - ing_____ in the month of_____ June,_____ A_____ small bird_____ sat_____ on an i - vy bunch_____ And the song he_____ sang_____ was the jug of punch._____ Too - ra loo - ra_____ loo,_____ too - ra loo - ra_____ lay,_____ Too - ra loo - ra_____ loo,_____ too - ra loo - ra_____ lay. A_____ *small bird_____ sat_____ on an i - vy bunch And the* *song he_____ sang_____ was the jug of punch.*

(Substitute last two lines of each verse in chorus as indicated in italics.)

What more diversion can a boy desire
Than to sit him down by an open fire,
And on his knee a tidy wench,
Aye, and on the table a jug of punch.

The learned doctors with all their art
Cannot cure the depression on the heart.
But even the cripple forgets his hunch
When he's snug outside of a jug of punch.

And when I'm dead and in my grave,
No costly tombstone will I crave.
Just lay me down in my native peat
With a jug of punch at my head and feet.

DRINK IT UP, MEN

Closing time for pubs in Ireland is 11:00 p.m. Guinness porter, commonly
known as 'stout', is a thick, dark brew that is consumed in prodigious
quantities throughout the country. Lord Iveagh (pronounced *ivy*) is the
owner of the brewery and wealthy beneficiary of a nation's thirst.

gDGBD **Traditional**

At the pub at the cross - roads there's

whis - key and beer, There's

bran - dy from Co - gnac that's fra - grant but

dear. But for kill - ing the

thirst and for rais - ing the gout, There's

noth - ing at all beats a pint of good stout.

Chorus:

Drink it up, men, It's

long af - ter ten!

Some folk o'er the water think bitters are fine
And others they swear by the juice of the vine.
But there's nothing that's brewed from the grape or the hop
Like the black liquidation with the froth on the top.

I've traveled in England, I've traveled in France,
At the sound of good music I'll sing or I'll dance.
So hear me then, mister, and pour me one more,
If I can't drink it up then throw me out the door.

It's Guinness's porter that has me this way.
Sure it's sweeter than buttermilk and stronger than tay.
But when in the morning I feel kind of rough,
My curse on Lord Iveagh who brews the damn stuff.

LITTLE BROWN JUG

This tune was published in 1869. Almost one hundred years later it was
on the Hit Parade in a swing arrangement by Glenn Miller.

gDGBD

Joseph Winner

My wife and I live all a - lone In a lit-tle brown hut we
call our own. She loves gin and I love rum.
Don't you know that we have fun. Ha, ha, ha,
you and me. Lit-tle brown jug, don't I love thee?
Ha, ha, ha, you and me. Lit-tle brown Jug, don't I love thee?

'Tis you who makes my friends my foes,
'Tis you who makes me wear old clothes.
But here you are so near my nose
So tip her up and down she goes.

When I go toiling on my farm,
Little brown jug under my arm,
Place her under a shady tree.
Little brown jug don't I love thee?

I lay in the shade of a big old tree,
Little brown jug in the shade of me,
I raise her up and give a pull,
Little brown jug's about half full.

The rose is red, my nose is too.
The violet's blue and so are you.
And I guess before I stop,
I'd better take another drop.

MOUNTAIN DEW

The classic American moonshine song, outrageous rhymes and all.

Traditional

Down the road here from me there's an old hol - low

tree Where you lay down a dol - lar or

two. You go round the

bend and you come back a - gain, There's a

jug full of that good old moun - tain dew.

Chorus:

Well, they call it that old moun - tain

dew And them that re -

fuse it are few. I'll

hush up my mug if you fill up my jug With that

good old moun - tain dew.

My uncle Nort, he's sawed-off and short,
He measures 'bout four foot two,
But he thinks he's a giant when you give him a pint
Of that good old mountain dew.

My old aunt Jane bought some brand-new perfume,
It had such a sweet-smelling "pew."
But to her surprise, when she had it analyzed
It was nothing but good old mountain dew.

The preacher rode by with his head heisted high,
Said his wife had come down with the flu.
He thought that I ort to give him a quart
Of that good old mountain dew.

My brother Bill's got a still on the hill
Where he runs off a gallon or two.
The buzzards in the sky get so drunk they can't fly,
From smelling that good old mountain dew.

THE MOONSHINER

This old fellow is the very embodiment of rugged individualism.

I've been a moon-shin-er for man-y a year. I've spent all my mon-ey on whis-key and beer. I'll go to some hol-low and set up my still And I'll sell you a gal-lon for a ten shil-ling bill.

Chorus:

I'm a ram-bler, I'm a gam-bler, I'm a long ways from home, And if you don't like me, well leave me a-lone. I'll eat when I'm hun-gry, and I'll drink when I'm dry, If the moon-shine don't kill me, I'll live till I die.

I'll go to some hollow in this country;
Ten gallons of wash, I can go on a spree.
No woman to follow, the world is all mine,
And I love none so well as I love the moonshine.

O Moonshine, O moonshine, O how I love thee,
You killed my old father but you'll never kill me.
God bless all moonshiners and bless all moonshine;
Its breath smells as sweet as the dew on the vine.

LOVERS FALSE AND TRUE

THE GIRL I LEFT BEHIND ME

This tune has been used for a great set of scurrilous verses called "The Wayward Boy."

Samuel Lover

Oh, ne'er shall I forget the night,
The stars were bright above me,
And gently lent their silvery light,
When first she vowed to love me.
But now I'm bound to Brighton camp,
Kind heaven, may favor find me,
And send me safely back again
To the girl I left behind me.

OH MY LITTLE DARLING

This song was collected on a Library of Congress field recording from
Thaddeus Willingham of Gulfport, Mississippi. A fine version, featuring
the banjo, has been recorded by County Down, a singing group from
Maine.

Traditional

Oh my lit - tle dar - ling, don't you weep and

cry. Some sweet day a - com - ing,

mar - ry you and I.

Up and down the railroad, 'cross the county line,
Pretty girls a-laughing, my wife is always crying.

Jimmy drives the wagon, Jimmy holds the line.
Kill yourself a-laughing, see them horses flying.

Oh my little darling, don't you weep and moan.
Some sweet day a-coming, take my baby home.

WILDWOOD FLOWER

This is the best-known of all the great Carter Family songs. Most
guitarists play this in the key of C. You can accomodate them by capoing
up five frets. Better yet, get them to learn it in G.

Oh he promised to love me, he promised to love,
To cherish me always, all others above.
I woke from dream and my idol was clay.
My passion for loving had vanished away.

He taught me to love him and called me his flower,
A blossom to cheer him through life's weary hour;
My poor heart is wondering, no misery can tell,
He left me no warning, no words of farewell.

I will dance, I will sing, and my life will be gay.
I will charm every heart in the crowd I survey.
I'll live yet to see him regret the dark hour
When he went and neglected his pale wildwood flower.

SHADY GROVE

This is usually the first tune banjo pickers learn in the G-modal tuning.
Musically it is a descendent of the British ballad, "Matty Groves."

gDGCD

Traditional

Shad - y___ Grove,_____ my lit - tle love,___

Shad - y___ Grove I say,_____

Shad - y___ Grove _____ my lit - tle love, I'm___

bound___ to___ go a - way. _____

Cheeks as red as a blooming rose,	When I was a little boy
Eyes of the prettiest brown.	I wanted a Barlow knife.
She's the darling of my heart,	Now I want little Shady Grove
Sweetest girl in town.	To say she'll be my wife.
I wish I had a big fine horse	Peaches in the summertime,
And corn to feed him on,	Apples in the fall,
And Shady Grove to stay at home	If I don't get the girl I love,
And feed him when I'm gone.	Don't want none at all.
Went to see my Shady Grove,	
She was standing in the door;	
Shoes and stockings in her hand	
And her little bare feet on the floor.	

THE NIGHTINGALE

There are many variants of this song throughout the British Isles. The outcome is always the same.

gDGBD

Traditional

As I was a - walk - ing one morn - ing in May, I spied a young cou - ple who fond - ly did stray. And one was a maid - en so sweet and so fair And the oth - er one was a sol - dier and a brave gren - a - dier.

Chorus: And they kissed so sweet and com-fort-ing as they clung to each oth-er. They went arm - in - arm down the road like sis - ter and broth-er. They went arm - in - arm down the road till they came to a stream And they both sat down to - geth-er, love, to hear the night - in - gale sing.

Then out of his knapsack he drew a fine fiddle
And he played her such merry tunes as you ever did hear.
He played her such merry tunes that the valley did ring,
And softly cried the fair maid, "Hear the nightingale sing."

"Now I'm off to India for seven long years,
Drinking wine a strong whiskey instead of pale beer.
And if ever I return again it'll be in the spring
And we'll both sit down together, love, to hear the nightingale sing."

"Oh soldier, oh soldier, will you marry me?"
"Oh no," cried the soldier, "however can that be?
For I've my own wife at home in my own country
And she's the fairest young thing that you ever did see."

JOHNNY TODD

Rounding Cape Horn in a raging gale wasn't the only danger a deep-water
sailor faced.

For a week she wept with sorrow, tore her hair, and wrung her hands
Till she met another sailor walking by the Liverpool sands.

"Why fair maid are you a-weeping for your Johnny gone to sea?
If you'll wed with me tomorrow I will kind and constant be.

"I will buy you sheets and blankets, I'll buy you a wedding ring.
You shall have a golden cradle for to rock the baby in."

Johnny Todd came home from sailing, sailing on the ocean wide,
And he found his fair and false one was another sailor's bride.

All young men who go a-sailing for to fight the foreign foe,
Do not leave your love like Johnny, marry her before your go.

ROLL IN MY SWEET BABY'S ARMS

This bluegrass standard makes a great knockdown style banjo tune. Play
it bold and boisterous.

gDGBD   **Traditional**

Chorus:

Roll in my sweet baby's arms,
Roll in my sweet baby's arms,
Gonna lay round this shack till the mail train comes back
Then I'll roll in my sweet baby's arms.

Sometimes there's a change in the ocean,
Sometimes there's a change in the sea,
Sometimes there's a change in my own truelove,
But there's never no change in me.

Mama's a ginger-cake baker,
Sister can weave and can spin,
Pa's got an interest in that old cotton mill,
Just watch that old money roll in.

Now where was you last Friday night
While I was locked up in that jail?
Walking the streets with another man,
Wouldn't even go my bail.

YOU ARE MY SUNSHINE

This was written by the Honorable James Davis, two-term Governor of
the state of Louisiana. Writing a love song should be a prerequisite for
holding public office.

Jimmie Davis and Charles Mitchell

You are my sun - shine,_____
_____ my on - ly sun - shine._____ You make me
hap - py,_____ when skies are gray._____
You'll nev - er know,_____ dear,_____ how much I
love_____ you._____ Please don't take_____ my
sun - shine a - way._____

The other night, dear, as I lay sleeping,
I dreamt I held you in my arms.
When I awoke, dear, I was mistaken
So I hung my head and cried.

MORE PRETTY GIRLS THAN ONE

I learned this song from a Rambling Jack Elliot record which features
Derroll Adams on banjo (Archive of Folk Music FS-210).

Chorus:
gDGBD

Traditional

There's more ____ pret-ty girls ____ than one,

More ____ pret-ty girls ____ than one.

In ev - ery ____ town ____ I ram - ble

round ____ There's more ____ pret-ty girls ____ than one.

Look down ____ that rail - road line, ____

See ____ that ____ train ____ roll by. ____

Train ____ rolls ____ by ____ with the wom-an ____ I

love, ____ Hang down ____ my head ____ and cry.

Look out across that sea
See the breakers swell.
How many loves have washed away
No human tongue can tell.

Look down that lonesome road
Before you travel on.
I'm leaving you this lonesome song
To sing when I am gone.

SPUNKY GALS

DICEY RILEY

'Pop' is Dublin slang for 'pawnshop'. Dicey was, for a time, the pride of
the streets of Dublin. Hail and farewell!

gDGBD   **Traditional**

Oh, poor old Di - cey Ri - ley she has tak - en to the

sup. Poor old Di - cey Ri - ley she will

nev - er give it up. It's off each morn - ing

to the pop And then she's read - y for an - oth - er lit - tle drop. Still the

heart of the role was Di - cey Ri - ley.

She'd walk along Fitzgibbon Street with an independent air,
Then it's down by Summerhill all as the people stare.
She'd say, "It's nearly half past one,
And time I had another little one."
Still the heart of the role was Dicey Riley.

Long years ago when men were men and fancied May Oblong,
And lovely Becky Cooper, and Maggie's Mary Wong;
One woman put them all to shame,
Just one was worthy of the name,
And the name of that same was Dicey Riley.

But time went catching up with her like many pretty whores;
It's after you along the street before you're out the door.
The balance weighed, their looks all fade.
But out of all that great brigade,
Still the heart of the role is Dicey Riley.

BLACK-EYED SUSIE

A simple but catchy melody. This is a good introductory song for double-C
tuning.

gCGCD

Traditional

All I____ want in____ this____ cre - a - tion,____

Pret - ty lit - tle wife____ and a big plan - ta - tion.

Chorus:

Hey,_____ pret - ty lit - tle black - eyed____ Sus - ie,

Hey,_____ pret - ty lit - tle black - eyed____ Sus - ie.

All I need to keep me happy,
Two little kids to call me pappy.

Some got drunk and some got boozy,
I went home with black-eyed Susie.

Love my wife, love my baby,
Love my biscuits sopped in gravy.

CINDY

Note the melodic use of the fifth string in the third from the last
measure.

gDGBD   **Traditional**

You ought to see my Cindy, She
lives a - way down south. Oh,
she's so sweet the hon - ey - bees
swarm a - round her mouth. Get a - long
home, Cin - dy, Cin - dy, Get a - long
home, Cin - dy, Cin - dy, Get a - long
home, Cin - dy, Cin - dy, I'll
mar - ry you some - day.

Oh, Cindy is a pretty girl;
Cindy is a peach.
She threw her arms around my neck
And hung on like a leech.

If I was a sugar tree
Standing in the town,
Every time my Cindy passed
I'd shake some sugar down.

I wish I was an apple
A-hanging on a tree,
Every time that Cindy passed
She'd take a bite of me.

HANDSOME MOLLY

Doc Watson sings and picks a nice version of this tune.

gDGBD

Traditional

Wish I___ was in Lon — don, or some oth - er sea - port town; ___ I'd set my___ foot in a steam - boat, I'd___ sail the___ o - cean round.___

While sailing on the ocean, while sailing on the sea,
I'd think of handsome Molly wherever she might be.

Don't you remember Molly, you gave me your right hand?
You said if you should marry, I would be the man.

Now you've broke your promise, you go with who you please;
While my poor heart is aching you're lying at your ease.

Hair as black as raven, eyes as black as coal,
Her cheeks were like the lilies out in the morning grown.

LITTLE MAGGIE

Most bluegrass players pick this in G tuning. The G-modal tuning brings
out more of the high, lonesome sound of this great old tune.

gDGCD   **Traditional**

O - ver   yon - der ___ stands ___ lit - tle ___

Mag - gie ___ With   a ___ dram ___ glass ___

in ___ her ___ hand. ___ She's a -

drink - ing ___ a - way ___ her ___ troub - les, ___ oh

Lord, ___ And ___ fool - ing ___ some   oth - er ___

man. ___

Sometimes I have a nickel,
Sometimes I have a dime,
And sometimes I have ten dollars
Just to buy little Maggie some wine.

The first time I seen little Maggie
She was sitting by the banks of the sea.
Had a forty-five strapped to her shoulder
And a banjo on her knee.

Pretty flowers were made for blooming,
Pretty stars were meant to shine,
Pretty girls were made for boys to love,
Little Maggie was made for mine.

Last time I seen little Maggie,
Had a suitcase in her hand.
She's going away for to leave me;
She's bound for some distant land.

THE MAID OF AMSTERDAM

Amsterdam is still a favorite liberty port for sailors.

Traditional

I took this maiden for a walk,
I took this maiden for a walk, and sweet and loving was our talk.

Her eyes are like two stars so bright,
Her eyes are like two stars so bright, her face is fair, her step is light.

Her cheeks are like the rosebud red,
Her cheeks are like the rosebud red; there's a wealth of hair upon her head.

I love this fair maid as my life,
I love this fair maid as my life and soon she'll be my darling wife.

POLLY WOLLY DOODLE

The only singer I've ever heard who really got to the heart of this song is
Leon Redbone (Warner Bros. BS-2888). His performance features Don
McLean on backup banjo.

gDGBD   **Traditional**

Well, I went down South for to see my Sal, Sing-ing

pol-ly wol-ly doo-dle all the day, My

Sal she is a spunk-y gal, Sing-ing

pol-ly wol-ly doo-dle all the day. Fare thee

well, fare thee well, Fare thee

well my fair-y fay. I'm

goin' to Lou'-si-an-a for to see my Sus-i-an-na Sing-ing

pol-ly wol-ly doo-dle all the day.

My Sal she is a maiden fair,
With curly eyes and laughing hair,

Grasshopper sitting on a railroad track,
Picking his teeth with a carpet tack,

BANJO PICKIN' GIRL

Also known as "Baby Mine," this was recorded years ago by Lily Mae
Ledford and the Coon Creek Girls. The tune has been traced back to a
popular love song of the 1880s.

Lily Mae Ledford

Goin'   round _____ this   world, _____ ba – by
mine, _____ I'm   goin'   round _____ this
world, _____ ba – by ___ mine, _____ I'm
goin'   round _____ this   world, _____ be   a   ban – jo   pick – in'
girl. _____ I'm _____ goin'   round _____ this   world, _____ ba – by
mine. _____

I'm goin' to Chattanooga, baby mine,
   Goin' to Chattanooga, baby mine,
  I'm goin' to Chattanooga
And from there I'm goin' to Cuba.
   Goin' to Chattanooga, baby mine.

I'm goin' to North Carolina, baby mine, *etc.*
And from there I'm goin' to China. *etc.*

I'm goin' to Tennessee, baby mine,
Don't you try to follow me.

I'm goin' across the ocean, baby mine,
If I don't change my notion.

If you ain't got no money, baby mine,
Get yourself another honey.

SWEET BETSY FROM PIKE

A deadpan performance will enhance the subtle humor of this American
classic.

gDGBD

Traditional

Oh, ____ do you re - mem - ber sweet ____

Bet - sy from Pike, ____ Who ____ crossed the big ____

moun - tains with ____ her lov - er, Ike, ____ With ____

two yoke of ____ cat - tle, and ____ one spot - ted ____

hog, ____ A ____ tall Shang - hai roos - ter, and an

Chorus:

old yal - ler dog? ____ Sing - ing, too - ra - la,

loo - ra - la, ____ loo - ra - la - la.

90

The Shanghai ran off and the cattle all died.
That morning the last piece of bacon was fried.
Poor Ike was discouraged and Betsy got mad.
The dog drooped his tail and looked wondrously sad.

They stopped at Salt Lake to inquire the way,
When Brigham declared that sweet Betsy could stay.
But Betsy got frightened and ran like a deer
While Brigham stood pawing the ground like a steer.

They soon reached the desert where Betsy gave out,
And down in the sand she lay rolling about
While Ike, half distracted, looked on with surprise,
Saying, "Betsy, get up, you'll get sand in your eyes."

This Pike County couple got married, of course.
But Ike became jealous, obtained a divorce.
Sweet Betsy, well satisfied, said with a shout,
"Good-by, you big lummox, I'm glad you backed out!"

LITTLE LIZA JANE

Don't be thrown off by the strum on the third beat of the "little Liza"
measures. That would be a good place to "strum the air."

gDGBD   **Traditional**

I got a gal who loves me so, _____ Lit-tle Liz - a

Jane, _____ Way down_ south in Bal - ti - more, _____

Lit - tle Liz - a Jane. _____ Oh, _____ E -

liz - a, _____ lit - tle Liz - a Jane, _____

Oh, _____ E - liz - a, _____ lit - tle Liz - a Jane. _____

Liza Jane looks good to me,
Sweetest gal I ever see,

I fell in love when I first saw,
Now I've got a mother-in-law,

House and lot in Baltimore,
Lots of children round the door,

I don't care how far I roam,
Very best place is home sweet home,

A PARCEL OF ROGUES

PADDY WEST

Mr. and Mrs. West ran a boarding house in Liverpool. Their training
program for sailors is a model of imaginative use of limited resources.

gDGBD

Traditional

As ___ I was a - walk - ing down Lon - don Road ___ I

came ___ to Pad - dy ___ West's house. ___ He ___

gave me ___ a ___ feed of A - mer - i - can ___ hash and he

called ___ it Liv - er - pool scouse. ___ He ___

said, "There's a ___ ship that's a - want - ing hands, ___ and ___

on her ___ you'll ___ quick - ly sign. ___ The

mate is ___ a ___ ty - rant, the bo - sun's worse, ___ but ___

she ___ will ___ suit ___ you ___ fine!" ___ **Chorus:** Put

on ___ your ___ dun - ga - ree jack - et ___ and

walk ___ up look - ing ___ your ___ best, ___ And

94

tell them— that— you're a poor sail - or lad——— that

came———— from Pad - dy— West. —————

Now when we had a feed, me boys, the wind began to blow,
He sent me up in the attic, the main royal for to stow,
But when I got up to the attic no main royal could I find
So I turned around to the window and I pulled the window blind.

Now Paddy he piped all hands on deck, their stations for to man.
His wife she stood in the doorway with a bucket in her hand,
Then Paddy, he cried, "Now let her rip!" and she flung the water away,
Saying, "Clew up your fore-topga'n's'l boys, she's takin' in the spray!"

"There's only one thing for you to do before you sail away.
Just step around the table with the bullocks on display,
And if they ask 'Were you ever at sea?' you can say 'Ten times round the Horn.'
You can tell them that you are a sailor since the day that you was born!"

OLD JOE CLARK

No one knows exactly who Old Joe was or where he came from, but his memory lives on in one of the best of all the old breakdown tunes. Hundreds of verses have been made up over the years chronicling the imaginary exploits of Mr. Clark. Try adding a few of your own to the legacy.

gDGBD   **Traditional**

Old Joe Clark, he had a mule,_____

Name was Mor - gan Brown._____

Ev - ery tooth in that mule's head Was____

six - teen____ inch - es round._____

Chorus:

Fare____ thee____ well,_____ Old Joe Clark,_____

Fare____ thee____ well I____ say.____

Fare____ thee____ well,_____ Old Joe Clark, I'm____

bound to____ go a - way._____

Old Joe Clark's a fine old man,
Tell you the reason why:
Keeps good likker round his house,
Good ole Rock and Rye.

Old Joe Clark he had a house,
Fifteen stories high.
Every room inside that house
Was filled with chicken pie.

I went down to Old Joe's house;
He invited me to supper.
I stumped my toe on the table leg
And stuck my nose in the butter.

Sixteen horses in my team;
The leaders they are blind.
Every time the sun goes down,
Pretty girl on my mind.

COTTON-EYED JOE

The country dancing craze set off by the movie, *Urban Cowboy*, made an
unlikely pop hit out of this old fiddle tune.

gDGBD   **Traditional**

Where   do   you   come   from?   Where   do   you   go?_____

Where   do   you   come   from,   Cot - ton - eyed   Joe?_____

Where   do   you   come   from,   Cot - ton - eyed   Joe?_____

Do you remember, a long time ago,
There was a man called Cotton-eyed Joe? *(twice)*

Old bull fiddle and a shoestring bow
Wouldn't play nothin' but Cotton-eyed Joe.

Play it fast or play it slow,
Don't play nothin' but Cotton-eyed Joe.

Could have been married a long time ago,
If it hadn't a-been for Cotton-eyed Joe.

OLD DAN TUCKER

Composed by the minstrel entertainer, Dan Emmett, and published in
1843, this song has long since been accorded the status of "folk song" by
generations of fiddlers and banjo pickers.

Daniel D. Emmett

Old Dan Tucker he got drunk,
Fell in the fire and kicked up a chunk.
Red hot coal got in his shoe.
Oh, my Lord, how the ashes flew!

Old Dan Tucker came to town,
Swinging the ladies round and round,
First to the right and then to the left,
Then to the girl that he loves best.

Old Dan Tucker's a fine old man,
Washed his face in a frying pan,
Combed his head with a wagon wheel,
Died with a toothache in his heel.

YANKEE DOODLE

This was the "theme song" of the American Revolutionary Army.

gDGBD

Traditional

Oh, Yank - ee Doo - dle went to town a -
rid - ing on a po - ny. He
stuck a feath - er in his hat and
called it "mac - a - ro - ni."

Chorus:

Yank - ee Doo - dle keep it up,
Yank - ee Doo - dle dan - dy,
Mind the mu - sic and the step and
with the girls be - han - dy.

Father and I went down to camp along with Captain Goodin,
There we saw the men and boys as thick as hasty puddin'.

There was General Washington upon a slapping stallion,
Giving orders to his men, I guess there was a million.

RAILROAD BILL

They don't come any more rambunctious than this old rounder.

Traditional

gDGBD

Rail - road _____ Bill, _____ Rail - road _____

Bill _____ He _____ nev - er worked _____ and _____

he _____ nev - er _____ will. _____ And it's ride, _____

ride, _____ ride. _____

Railroad Bill was a mighty mean man,
Shot the midnight lantern out the brakeman's hand.

Railroad Bill took my wife,
Said if I didn't like it he would take my life.

Railroad Bill, Railroad Bill,
Lives up top of Railroad Hill.

MURDER AND FOUL PLAY

FRANKIE AND JOHNNY

I always thought bartenders were souls of discretion. Maybe Johnny
didn't leave a tip.

Traditional

Frank - ie and John - ny were sweet - hearts,

Oh, Lord - y, how they could love.

Swore to be true to each oth - er, Just as

true as the stars a - bove. He was her

man, but he was do - ing her

wrong.

Frankie went down to the corner
Just for a bucket of beer.
She said, "Please, mister bartender,
Has my loving Johnny been here?
    He was my man, but he's a-doing me wrong."

"I don't want to tell you no stories,
Don't want to tell you no lies,
But I saw your man about an hour ago
With a gal named Nellie Bligh.
    He was your man, but he's a-doing you wrong."

Frankie went down to the hotel,
She didn't go there for fun;
Underneath her kimono
She carried a forty-four gun.
    He was her man, but he was doing her wrong.

Frankie looked over the transom
To see what she could spy.
There sat Johnny on the sofa
Just loving up Nellie Bligh.
    He was her man, but he was doing her wrong.

Frankie got down from that high stool;
She didn't want to see no more.
Rooty-toot-toot three times she shoot
Right through that hardwood door.
    He was her man, but he was doing her wrong.

Sixteen rubber-tired carriages,
Sixteen rubber-tired hacks,
They take poor Johnny to the graveyard,
Ain't gonna bring him back.
    He was her man, but he was doing her wrong.

Frankie she said to the sheriff,
"What do you reckon they'll do?"
Sheriff he said to Frankie,
"It's the 'lectric chair for you."
    He was her man, but he was doing her wrong.

This story has no moral,
This story has no end.
This story only goes to show
That there ain't no good in men.
    He was her man, but he done her wrong.

TOM DOOLEY

The Kingston Trio's landmark recording of this ballad was based on Frank
Proffit's version. This arrangement is from the singing of Doc Watson
who learned it from his mother. The facts behind the ballad seem to
indicate that Laura Foster was killed by a woman named Annie Melton.
Tom Dooley, a Civil War hero and, it is said, a good fiddler, buried the
body and was tried and hanged for murder. Sheriff Grayson later married
Annie, remaining ignorant of her crime until she confessed it to him on
her deathbed.

You took her on the hillside
To beg her to be your wife.
You took her on the hillside,
You stabbed her with your knife.

You dug her grave four feet long,
You dug it three feet deep,
You rolled the cold clay over her
And tromped it with your feet.

"I know they're gonna hang me,
Tomorrow I'll be dead,
Though I never even harmed a hair
On poor little Laurie's head.

"In this world and one more,
Reckon where I'll be.
If it wasn't for Sheriff Grayson
I'd have been in Tennessee.

"Take my fiddle off the wall,
Play it all you please,
For at this time tomorrow
It'll be no use to me.

"At this time tomorrow
Reckon where I'll be,
Down in yonder holler
Hanging on a white oak tree."

JESSE JAMES

Jesse was the most famous outlaw of the lot; thanks to Billy Gashade,
who wrote the ballad that has perpetuated the legend of this frontier
Robin Hood.

Billy Gashade

Jes - se James was a lad who killed man-y a
man; He robbed the Glen - dale
train. And the peo - ple they did
say for man - y miles a - way, It was
robbed by Frank and Jes - se James.

Chorus:
Poor Jes - se had a wife to
mourn for his life; Three chil - dren
they were brave. But that
dirt - y lit - tle cow - ard who shot Mis - ter How-ard has
laid poor Jes - se in his grave.

Jesse James was a man, a friend to the poor;
He'd never see a man suffer pain.
With his brother Frank, he robbed the Chicago bank
And stopped the Glendale train.

It was his brother Frank that robbed the Gallatin bank
And carried the money from the town.
It was in that very place they had a little race,
For they shot Captain Sheets to the ground.

It was on a Saturday night and Jesse was at home
Talking with his family brave.
Robert Ford came along like a thief in the night
And laid poor Jesse in his grave.

Jesse went to his rest with his hand upon his breast,
The devil will be upon his knee.
He was born one day in the county of Clay,
And came from a solitary race.

PRETTY POLLY

A beautiful modal melody. Woody Guthrie used a variant of it for
"Pastures of Plenty."

gDGB♭D

Traditional

Pol - ly,___ pret - ty___ Pol - ly, come

go a - long___ with ___ me. ___

Pol - ly,___ pret - ty___ Pol - ly, come

go a - long___ with___ me, ___ Be -

fore___ we___ get___ mar - ried some

pleas - ure___ to___ see. ___

She jumped on behind him and away they did go, *(twice)*
Over the hills and the valley below.

They went a little farther and what did they spy,
But a new dug grave with a spade lying by.

"Oh Willie, oh Willie, I'm afraid of your ways,
I'm so afraid you will lead me astray."

"Polly, pretty Polly, you've guessed about right,
I dug on your grave for most of last night.

"There's no time to talk now, there's no time to stand,"
He drew out his knife all in his right hand.

He stabbed her in the heart and the blood it did flow,
And into her grave pretty Polly did go.

He threw on some dirt and he started for home,
Leaving nothing behind but the wild birds to moan.

Now a debt to the devil Willie must pay,
For killing pretty Polly and running away.

WILD BILL JONES

A classic mountain melody, first recorded by banjoist Samantha
Bumgarner. It is set in the open-D tuning.

Traditional

Chorus:

So pass around that long-neck bottle
And we'll all go on a spree.
For today was the last of Wild Bill Jones
And tomorrow is the last of me.

He said his age it is twenty-one,
Too old for to be controlled.
I pulled my revolver from my side;
I destroyed that poor boy's soul.

He reeled and he staggered and he fell to the ground
And he gave one dying groan.
I threw my arms around my darlin's neck,
Saying, "Baby, won't you please come home."

They sent me to prison for twenty long years;
This poor boy longs to be free.
But Wild Bill Jones and that long-neck bottle
Has made a ruin of me.

JOHN HARDY

The phrase "desperate little man" deprives this song of the heroic
dimension to be found in most outlaw ballads. Nonetheless, it has a good
melody which Woody Guthrie used for his synopsis of *The Grapes of
Wrath*, "The Ballad of Tom Joad."

John Hardy run for the old state line;
He thought he would go free.
But a man walked up and took him by the arm,
Saying, "Johnny walk along with me,
Johnny walk along with me."

The first one to visit John Hardy in his cell
Was a little girl dressed in blue.
She came on down to that old jail cell,
Saying, "Johnny, I've been true to you, Lord knows,
Johnny I've been true to you."

The next one to visit John Hardy in his cell
Was a little girl dressed in red.
She came down to that old jail cell,
Saying, "Johnny, I had rather see you dead, Lord knows,
Johnny I had rather see you dead."

John Hardy stood in his old jail cell,
The tears running down from his eyes.
He said, "I've been the death of many a poor boy,
But my six-shooter never told a lie, God knows,
My six-shooter never told a lie."

THE BANKS OF THE OHIO

This is a good tune for adding a high and/or low harmony part.

Chorus:

Then only say that you'll be mine,	I held a knife against her breast,	I started home 'twixt twelve and one.
And in on other's arms entwine,	As into my arms she pressed.	I cried, "My God, what have I done?
Down beside where the waters flow,	She cried, "Willie, don't murder me,	I've killed the only woman I love
Down by the banks of the Ohio.	I'm not prepared for eternity."	Because she would not be my bride."

109

BUFFALO SKINNERS

Structurally similar to a number of ballads, such as "Canaday-I-O," Irwin
Silber calls this "perhaps the greatest Western song of them all." This
arrangement is in the G-minor tuning.

Come all you old-time cowboys and listen to my song; And please do not grow weary, I'll not detain you long; Concerning some wild cowboys who did agree to go And spend a summer pleasant on the trail of the buffalo.

'Twas in the town of Jacksboro in the spring of '73,
A man by the name of Crego came stepping up to me,
Said, "How do you do, young feller, and how would you like to go,
And spend the summer pleasant on the trail of the buffalo?"

Me being out of work right then, to Crego I did say,
"This going out on the buffalo range depends upon the pay.
But if you pay good wages and transportation too,
I think, sir, I will go with you to the range of the buffalo."

It's now we've crossed Pease River, our troubles have begun.
The first damned tail I went to rip, Christ! how I cut my thumb!
While skinning the damned old stinkers our lives they had no show,
For the Indians watched to pick us off while skinning the buffalo.

He fed us on such sorry chuck I wished myself most dead.
'Twas old jerked beef and coffee with wormy sourbread.
Pease River water's salty, to drink it I couldn't go.
O God! I wished I'd never come to the range of the buffalo.

Our working day was sun to sun; the nights we did all dread,
For all we had to sleep on was a buffalo robe for a bed.
The fleas and lice they worked on us; oh, boys, they were not slow.
You can bet there's no worse hell on earth than the trail of the buffalo.

The season being near over, old Crego he did say
The crowd had been too wasteful, was in debt to him that day.
We coaxed him and we begged him and still it was no go,
So we left old Crego's bones to bleach on the trail of the buffalo.

It's now we've crossed Pease River and homeward we are bound.
No more in that damned country shall ever we be found.
Go home to wives and sweethearts, tell others not to go,
For God's forsaken all who go on the trail of the buffalo.

CAPTAIN KIDD

This is musically identical to the ballad, "Sam Hall." An alternate title to
this might be, "Mamas, Don't Let Your Babies Grow Up to Be Pirates."

Oh, my name is Cap - tain Kidd, As I
sailed, as I sailed. Oh, my name is Cap - tain
Kidd, As I sailed. Oh, my
name is Cap - tain Kidd, God's laws I did for -
bid, And most wick - ed - ly I did, As I
sailed, as I sailed, And most wick - ed - ly I
did, As I sailed.

My parents taught me well
To shun the gates of hell,
But against them I rebelled,

I murdered William Moore
And left him in his gore,
Forty leagues from shore,

And being cruel still,
My gunner I did kill,
And his precious blood did spill,

Now to Execution Dock
    I must go, I must go.
To Execution Dock
    I must go.
To Execution Dock,
Lay my head upon the block,
No more the laws I'll mock,
    As I hang, as I hang.
No more the laws I'll mock,
    As I hang.

112

LONG STEEL RAILS

THE WABASH CANNONBALL

If you can imitate a train whistle this is the song for it. This was a
signature tune of the great country singer, Roy Acuff.

gDGBD Traditional

From the great At - lan - tic O - cean____ to the____ wide Pa - cif - ic

shore,_____ From the____ queen of____ flow - ing moun - tains____ to the

south belle by the shore,_____ She's a - might - y____ tall and hand - some,_____ well

known by____ one and all,_____ She's the mod - ern___ com - bi - na - tion___ called the

Chorus:

Wa - bash____ Can - non - ball._____ Oh, lis - ten____ to the

jin - gle,____ the rum - ble,__ and the roar,_____ As she glides a - long the

wood - lands, through the hills, and__ by the shore.____ Hear the might - y____ rush of

en - gines,__ hear that__ lone - some__ ho - bo's call. You're rid - ing__ through the

jun - gles__ on the Wa - bash__ Can - non - ball._____

The Eastern states are dandy the people always say.
From New York to St. Louis and Chicago, by the way,
To the hills of Minnesota where the rippling waters fall,
No changes need be taken on the Wabash Cannonball.

So here's to Daddy Claxton, may his name forever stand,
And always be remembered round the courts of Alabam'.
His earthly race is over and the curtain round him falls;
We'll carry him to Dixie on the Wabash Cannonball.

FREIGHT TRAIN

This was written by Elizabeth Cotten when she was a young girl. Several
generations of fingerstyle guitarists have cut their musical teeth on her
tune.

gDGBD   **Elizabeth Cotten**

Freight train, freight train go - in' so
fast, Freight train, freight train
go - in' so fast Please, don't
tell what train I'm on So they
won't know where I've - gone.

When I'm dead and in my grave,
No more good times here I'll crave.
Place the stones at my head and feet
And tell 'em I'm gone to sleep.

When I die, Lord, bury me deep,
Way down on old Chestnut Street,
So I can hear old Number Nine
As she goes rolling by.

115

JOHN HENRY

The greatest of American folk heroes commemorated in the greatest of
American ballads.

gDGBD   **Traditional**

When John Hen - ry was a

lit - tle ba - by boy, Just a - sit - tin' on his

dad - dy's knee, He

picked up a ham - mer and a lit - tle piece of

steel, Say - in', "Ham - mer's - gon - na be the death of

me, Lord, Lord, Ham - mer's gon - na

be the death of me."

The captain said to John Henry,
"Gonna bring that steam drill round.
Gonna bring that steam drill out on the job,
Gonna whup that steel on down." *(twice)*

John Henry said to his captain,
"Lord, a man ain't nothin' but a man.
But before I let that steam drill beat me down,
I'll die with my hammer in my hand."

John Henry said to his shaker,
"Shaker, why don't you sing?
Cause I'm swinging thirty pounds from my hips on down;
Just listen to that cold steel ring."

Now the captain said to John Henry,
"I believe that mountain's caving in."
John Henry said right back to the captain,
"Ain't nothin' but my hammer suckin' wind."

Now the man that invented the steam drill,
He thought he was mighty fine.
But John Henry drove fifteen feet,
Steam drill only made nine.

John Henry hammered in the mountains;
His hammer was striking fire.
But he worked so hard it broke his poor heart
And he laid down his hammer and he died.

Now John Henry had a little woman,
Her name it was Polly Ann.
She picked up his hammer and took it to the line;
Polly Ann drove steel like a man.

Now they took John Henry to the graveyard,
They buried him in the sand.
Every locomotive come roarin' by
Says, "There lies a steel-drivin' man."

BOUND TO RIDE

This is a favorite among bluegrass pickers. Play it with a hard-driving
beat.

Com - ing__ down from__ Ten - nes - see,_____ rid - ing__ on__ the__
line,_____ Stud-y-ing__ 'bout that__ gal of mine,_____
could - n't__ keep from cryin'._____ Hon - ey_____ babe, I'm__
bound to ride,_____ don't you want__ to__ go?_____

Going to Atlanta just to look around.
Then, if things don't suit me, I'll find another town.

Working on a railroad, saving all I can,
Looking for a woman that ain't got no man.

If I die a railroad man, bury me 'neath the ties
So I can see old Number Nine as she goes rolling by.

See that train a-coming, coming 'round the bend;
Goodbye, little darling, I'm on my way again.

NINE HUNDRED MILES

Here is a beautiful melody, full of that high, lonesome sound. The banjo is
tuned to D-minor.

aDFAD   **Traditional**

I am walk-ing down this track, I got tears in my eyes, Trying to read a let-ter from my home. If this train runs me right, I'll be home to-mor-row night. Lord, I'm nine hun-dred miles from my home And I hate to hear that lone-some whis-tle blow.

118

This train I ride on is a hundred coaches long;
You can hear her whistle blow a hundred miles.
    If this train runs me right, *etc.*

I will pawn you my wagon, I will pawn you my team,
I will pawn you my watch and my chain.

BEEN ALL AROUND THIS WORLD

In which is presented a somewhat jaundiced view of matrimony.

gDGBD
                                                Traditional

Dig - gin' on the new rail - road in the mud up to my knees, Dig - gin' on the new rail - road in the mud up to my knees. Dig - gin' for old John Hen - ry and he's so hard to please. I been all a - round this world.

Once I had an old gray mule name was Morgan Brown, *(twice)*
Every tooth in that mule's head was sixteen inches round.

Single girl, single girl, dress you wear's so fine,
Wait till you get married, go raggedy all the time.

Where'd you get that pretty dress, shoes that look so fine?
Got my dress from a railroad man, shoes from a driver in the mine.

119

NEW RIVER TRAIN

This is a great party song. Toss it around the circle and improvise the
verses.

Traditional

I'm rid-ing___ on that___ new___ riv-er train,_____ Rid-ing___ on that___ new___ riv-er train._____ Same___ old ___ train ___ that ___ brought ___ me here ___ Gon-na take___ me a-way___ a-gain.___

Darling, you can't love one,
  Darling, you can't love one.
You can't love one and have any fun.
  Darling, you can't love one.

Darling, you can't love two,
You can't love two and still be true.

Darling, you can't love three,
You can't love three and still love me.

Darling, you can't love four,
You can't love four and love any more.

Darling, you can't love five,
You can't love five and get honey from my hive.

Darling, you can't love six,
You can't love six 'cause that kind of love don't mix.

Darling, you can't love seven,
You can't love seven and expect to get to heaven.

Darling, you can't love eight,
You can't love eight and get through the Pearly Gates.

Darling, you can't love nine,
You can't love nine and still be mine.

SHOUTING THE BLUES

CRAWDAD

This sassy number is often sung as a play-party song. With different
lyrics it is known as "Sweet Thing."

gDGBD

Traditional

You get a line,_____ I'll get a pole,_____ hon-ey,_____

You get a line,_____ I'll__ get a pole,_____

babe,_____ You get a line,_____

I'll__ get a pole,_____ We'll__ go__ down to the craw-dad hole,_____

Hon-ey,_____ oh sug-ar__ ba-by mine._____

Along come a man with a sack on his back, honey, *etc.*
Packin' all the crawdads he can pack,

What you gonna do when the lake goes dry, honey?
Sit on the bank and watch the crawdads die,

What you gonna do when the crawdads die, honey?
Sit on the bank until I cry,

I heard the duck say to the drake, honey,
There ain't no crawdads in this lake,

CARELESS LOVE

Folklorists say that this is one of the oldest blues. The theme is as old as humanity.

I love my mama and papa too, *(three times)*
I'd leave them both to go with you.

Sorrow, sorrow to my heart,
Since me and my truelove had to part.

What, oh what will mama say,
When she learns I've gone astray.

SALTY DOG BLUES

This follows a classic chord progression which has been used for hundreds
of songs, but none more popular than good old "Salty Dog."

gDGBD   Chorus: **Traditional**

Let me be your salt-y dog Or

I don't want to be your man at all.

Hon-ey let me be your salt-y

dog.

Standing on the corner with the low-down blues,
Great big hole in the bottom of my shoes.
    Honey, let me be your salty dog.

Look here, Sal, I know you,
With a low-down slipper and a brogan shoe.
    Honey, let me be your salty dog.

Down in the wildwood sitting on a log,
Finger on the trigger, eye on a hog.
    Honey, let me be your salty dog.

Pulled the trigger, the gun said go,
The shot rung over in Mexico.
    Honey, let me be your salty dog.

LONG JOURNEY HOME

Bluegrass pickers know this as "Two Dollar Bill." It is closely related to
"Going down the Road" and "Gotta Travel On."

gDGBD   **Traditional**

Lost all my mon-ey but a two-dol-lar

bill, Two-dol-lar bill, boys.

two-dol-lar bill. Lost all my

124

mon - ey____ but a____ two - dol - lar bill,____ I'm____

on____ my____ long____ jour - ney home.____

My baby left me, she's gone away,
She's gone away, boys, she's gone away.
My baby left me, she's gone away.
I'm on my long journey home.

I'm leaving on the evening train, count the days I'm gone,
Count the days I'm gone, boys, count the days I'm gone.
I'm leaving on the evening train, count the days I'm gone.
I'm on my long journey home.

GOIN' DOWN THE ROAD FEELIN' BAD

Woody Guthrie made this the theme song of the displaced and the
dispossessed: Dust Bowl refugees, migrant workers, hoboes, and
wandering musicians.

gDGBD

Traditional

Go - in' down____ the road____ feel - in' bad,____

Well, I'm go - in'____ down the____ road____ feel - in'

bad,____ Yes, I'm go - in'____ down the____

road____ feel - in' bad,____ Lord,____ Lord,____ And I

ain't gon - na____ be treat - ed____ this a - way.____

Takes a ten-dollar shoe to fit my feet, *etc.*

Cause your two-dollar shoes hurt my feet,

I'm goin' where the weather suits my clothes,

WORRIED MAN BLUES

Chances are that somewhere, even as you read these words, a bluegrass
band is playing this song.

gDGBD   Traditional

It takes a ___ wor - ried man ___ to

sing a ___ wor - ried song, ___ It ___

takes a ___ wor - ried man ___ to ___

sing a ___ wor - ried song, ___ I'm ___ wor - ried

now, ___ but I

won't be wor - ried long. ___

I went across the river and laid me down to sleep, *(three times)*
When I woke up, I had shackles on my feet.

Twenty-nine links of chain around my leg,
On each link, an initial of my name.

I asked the judge, what might be my fine,
Twenty-one years on the Rocky Mountain line.

SUGAR BABE

This is a favorite among blues guitarists. Mance Lipscomb, a Texas
songster, recorded an eight-bar version of this sardonic lament.

Sug - ar babe, what's the mat-ter with you?_____ You don't treat me like you

used__ to do._____ Sug - ar babe, it's all _____ o - ver

now. _____ Sug - ar babe, I'm__

tired__ of you,_____ Run - nin' round__ with some - bod - y new._____

Sug - ar babe,_____ sug - ar__ babe, It's all _____ o - ver

now. _____

All I want my baby to do,
Make five dollars and give me two.
Sugar babe, it's all over now.
Sugar babe, you're making me blue,
Takin' up with somebody new.
Sugar babe, sugar babe,
It's all over now.

FISHIN' BLUES

From an early field recording by Henry "Ragtime Texas" Thomas, this has
become one of the most popular good-time blues songs. Taj Mahal has
recorded it, adding a couple of verses of his own.

gDGBD

Henry Thomas

Ba - by been a - fish - in' _____ all of the time; _____
I'm a - go - in' fish - in' _____ too. _____
Bet _____ your _____ life, _____ your _____ sweet wife, _____ gon - na
catch more _____ fish than you. _____ Well, an - y fish bites if you
got _____ good bait. _____ Here's a lit - tle tip that I would
like to re - late: _____ With _____ my _____ pole _____ and _____ my _____ line, _____
I'm a - go - in' fish - in', _____ yes I'm go - in' fish - in', And my
ba - by go - in' fish - in' _____ too. _____

128

ALL GOD'S CRITTERS

THE COO-COO

This old tune has that haunting sound so often heard in traditional music.
The banjo is tuned to G-minor.

Traditional

Oh,___ the___ coo - coo,_____ she's___ a___

pret - ty bird,_____ And she____

war - bles _____ as _____ she

flies. _____ But_____ she____

nev - er_____ hol - lers____

coo - coo _____ Till the_____

fourth _____ day _____ of _____ Ju -

ly. _____

Jack of diamonds, jack of diamonds,
I know you of old.
You robbed my poor pockets
Of my silver and my gold.

I've played cards in England,
I've played cards in Spain,
And I'll bet you five dollars
I'll beat you this game.

Gonna build me a log cabin
On the mountain so high
So I can see my little love
As she goes riding by.

Oh, the coo-coo, she's a pretty bird.
Don't I wish she was mine?
She'd never drink water,
She'd always drink wine.

OLD MOLLY HARE

A fun old fiddle tune with typical nonsense verses.

Old___ Mol - ly Hare,_____ what you do - in' there?_____

Sit - tin' by the fire - side a - smok - in' my ci - gar._____

Old Molly Hare, what you doin' there?
Runnin' through the briar patch hard as I can tear.

Jump up, Molly now, yonder comes a bear,
Runnin' down the hillside hard as he can tear.

Step back, step back, daddy shot a bear,
Shot him through the eye and never touched a hair.

Old Molly Hare, what you doin' there?
Sittin' by the butter dish pickin' out a hair.

TURKEY IN THE STRAW

This is one of the most familiar of all the old minstrel tunes. It was
published in 1834 and authorship has been claimed by both Bob Farrell
and George Washington Dixon.

gCGCE   **Traditional**

Well, I had a lit-tle chick-en and she had a wood-en leg, She's the

fin-est lit-tle chick-en that has ev-er laid an egg, Well, she

laid a lot more eggs than an-y chick-en on the farm, But an-

oth-er lit-tle drink would-n't do her an-y harm.

Chorus:

Tur-key in the hay, in the hay, hay, hay,

Tur-key in the straw, in the straw, straw, straw,

Pick 'em up, shake 'em up, an-y way at all, And we'll

pick a lit-tle tune called "Tur-key in the Straw."

Well, I hitched up the wagon and I drove down the road,
With a two-horse wagon and a four-horse load.
Well, I cracked my whip and the lead horse sprung,
And I said goodbye to the wagon tongue.

Well, if frogs had wings and snakes had hair,
And automobiles went a-flying through the air,
And if watermelons grew on a huckleberry vine,
We'd have winter in the sunny summertime.

MOLE IN THE GROUND

This tune was recorded years ago by Bascomb Lamar Lunsford on Folkways FP-40. Variants are "My Doney Where You Been So Long?" (Ola Belle Reed on *Old Time Banjo in America*) and "Omie Let Your Bangs Hang Down" (Gaither Carlton on *More Clawhammer Banjo*).

gCGCE   **Traditional**

I wish I was a lizard in the tree, *(twice)*
If I's a lizard in that tree
I would have you there with me,
  I wish I was a lizard in the tree.

I wish I was a turtle in the pond,
If I's a turtle in that pond
I would stay there all day long,
  I wish I was a turtle in the pond.

LITTLE BIRDIE

This is arranged in the standard-C tuning. Many old-timers play this in
the so-called "Little Birdie tuning": eCGAD or gCGAD.

Lit - ltc bird - ie, _____ lit - tle ___ bird - ie, _____ Come _____ sing _____ to me _____ your _____ song. _____ Got ___ a ___ short _____ time _____ for ___ to ___ stay _____ here _____ And ___ a ___ long _____ time to ___ be ___ gone. _____

Little birdie, little birdie,
What makes you fly so high?
It's because I am a true little bird
And I do not fear to die.

Little birdie, little birdie,
What makes your wing so blue?
It's because I've been grieving,
Grieving after you.

Little birdie, little birdie,
What makes your head so red?
After all that I have been through
It's a wonder I ain't dead.

GO TELL AUNT RHODY

Sounds like the fox paid a visit to Rhody's farm. She ought to sponge up
all the tears and make a water bed.

Old gander's weeping, *(three times)*
Because his wife is dead.

The goslings are mourning,
Because their mother's dead.

She died in the mill pond,
Standing on her head.

THE FOX

Bringing home the bacon for a family of twelve keeps a fox on the run.

gDGBD   Traditional

Oh, the fox went out on a chil - ly night, Prayed to the moon to give him light, For he'd man - y a mile to go that night Be - fore he reached the town - o, town - o, town - o, He'd man - y a mile to go that night Be - fore he reached the town - o.

136

He ran till he came to a great big pen,
The ducks and the geese were kept therein,
Said, "A couple of you will grease my chin
Before I leave this town-o, *etc.*

He grabbed the gray goose by the neck,
Slung the little one over his back,
He didn't mind the quack, quack, quack,
And the legs all dangling down-o,

Old mother pitter-patter jumped out of bed,
Out of the window she stuck her head,
Crying, "John, John, the gray goose is gone,
And the fox is on the town-o,

John, he went to the top of the hill,
Blew his horn both loud and shrill.
The fox, he said, "I better run with my kill,
They'll soon be on my trail-o,

He ran till he came to his cozy den,
There were the little ones, eight, nine, ten,
They said, "Dad, you better go back again,
Cause it must be a mighty fine town-o,

Then the fox and his wife, without any strife,
Cut up the goose with fork and knife.
They never had such a supper in their life
And the little ones chewed on the bones-o,

CLUCK OLD HEN

One of the best G-modal tunes. Listen to Kyle Creed and Fred Cockerham play this on fiddle and banjo (*Clawhammer Banjo* County 701). The sound you hear is the quintessence of old-time country music.

gDGCD

Traditional

My old hen's a ____ good old hen, ____

She lays eggs for the rail - road men, ____

Some - times ____ eight and ____ some - times ____ ten, ____

That's ____ e - nough ____ for the rail - road ____ men. ____

Cluck old hen, ____ cluck ____ and sing, ____

Ain't laid an egg ____ since late ____ last spring. ____

Cluck old ____ hen, ____ cluck ____ and ____ squall, ____

Ain't laid an egg ____ since ____ late ____ last ____ fall. ____

SWING YOUR PARTNER

BUFFALO GALS

Authorship has been ascribed to minstrel entertainer John "Cool White" Hodges around 1844. Can be sung about gals from any town, state, or country you choose.

gDGBD

John Hodges

As I was walk - ing down the street,_____

Down the street,_____ down the street, A_____

pret - ty_____ maid__ I chanced__ to meet And_____

she was___ fair___ to___ see._____ Oh,

Buf - fa - lo gals won't you come out___ to - night, Won't you

come out___ to - night, won't you come out___ to - night?_____

Buf - fa - lo_____ gals___ won't you come out___ to - night And_____

dance____ by the light of the moon?_____

140

I asked her would she have some talk,
  Have some talk, have some talk.
Her feet covered up the whole sidewalk
As she stood close by me.

I asked her would she have a dance,
  Have a dance, have a dance.
I thought that I might get a chance
To shake a foot with her.

I'd like to make that gal my wife,
  Gal my wife, gal my wife.
I'd be happy all my life
If I had her by me.

FLY AROUND, MY PRETTY LITTLE MISS

Some prefer to sing "fly around my blue-eyed gal." Blue-eyed gals might
prefer to sing "brown-eyed boy." A great old tune any way you take it.

gDGBD   **Traditional**

Fly____ a - round, my____ pret - ty lit - tle miss,____

Fly a - round, my dai - sy,____

Fly____ a - round, my____ pret - ty lit - tle miss, You____

al - most____ drive me cra - zy.____

Once I had a fortune,
Laid it in a trunk,
Lost it all a-gamblin',
One night when I got drunk.

Wish I was on a mountaintop,
Sittin' in a chair,
One arm round my whiskey jug,
The other round my dear.

Every day and Sunday too,
Seems so dark and hazy,
Thinkin' 'bout my blue-eyed gal,
She's done run me crazy.

DOWN THE ROAD

This tune is similar to "Ida Red" and the Bob Wills favorite, "Stay All Night."

Traditional

Down the road 'bout a mile or two,

Lives a little girl named Pearly Blue.

Hair is red and her eyes are brown,

Prettiest girl in the whole darn town.

Chorus:

Down the road, down the road,

Got a little pretty girl down the road.

Any old time you want to know
Where I'm heading, it's down the road
To see the girl that's on my mind;
You'll find me there most any time.

Every day and Sunday too,
I go to see my Pearly Blue.
Before you hear the rooster crow,
You'll see me heading down the road.

SALLY ANN

Drive the rhythm of this tune by coming down strong on the downbeats
(the first beat of each measure).

Traditional

Ev - er see a musk - rat. Sal - ly Ann,

Pick - in' a banjo, Sal - ly Ann,

Drag - gin' his slick tail through the sand?

I'm a - gon - na mar - ry you, Sal - ly Ann.

Chorus:

I'm gon - na - mar - ry you Sal, Sal,

I'm gon - na mar - ry you, Sal - ly Ann.

Going to the wedding, Sally Ann, *(twice)*
Sift that meal and save your bran,
I'm going home with Sally Ann.

Shake that little foot, Sally Ann,
Great big wedding up, Sally Ann,
I'm going home with Sally Ann.

Pass me the brandy, Sally Ann,
I'm going 'way with Sally Ann,
Great big wedding up, Sally Ann.

SKIP TO MY LOU

The best-known of the frontier era play-party songs, and a fine singalong
for kids.

gDGBD   **Traditional**

G

Skip, _____ skip, _____ skip to my Lou, _____

D7

Skip, _____ skip, _____ skip to my Lou, _____

G

Skip, _____ skip, _____ skip to my Lou, _____

D7   h   **G**

Skip to my Lou my dar - ling. _____

G

Lost my part - ner, what'll__ I do? _____

D7

Lost my part - ner, what'll__ I do? _____

G

Lost my part - ner, what'll__ I do? _____

D7   h   **G**

Skip to my Lou my dar - ling. _____

144

Lost my partner, what'll I do? *(three times)*
Skip to my Lou my darling.

I'll get another one prettier than you, *etc.*

Little red wagon painted blue,

Flies in the buttermilk, shoo, shoo, shoo,

Cat's in the cream jar, what'll I do?

SALLY GOODIN

Earl Scruggs picks the classic bluegrass version of this old favorite
(Columbia CS-8364).

Had a piece of pie,_____ had a piece of pud - din'; ___

Gave it all a - way___ just to see Sal - ly Good - in. ___

Looked down the road, seen my Sally comin',
Though to my soul I'd kill myself a-runnin'.

Love a 'tater pie, love an apple puddin',
Love a little gal they call Sally Goodin.

Goin' up the mountain and marry little Sally;
Raise corn on the hill and the devil in the valley.

CAN'T YOU DANCE THE POLKA?

I wonder if Tiffany's has any of those fifty-cent earrings left?

Traditional

As I walked down on Broadway one eve-ning in Ju-ly, I met a maid who asked my trade; "A sail-or John," says I. Then a-way, you San-ty, my dear An-nie. Oh, you New York girls, can't you dance the pol-ka?

To Tiffany's I took her, I did not mind expense,
I bought her two gold earrings, they cost me fifty cents.

Says she, "You limejuice sailor, now see me home you may."
But when we reached her cottage door she unto me did say:

"My flashman he's a Yankee, with his hair cut short behind,
He wears a tarry jumper and he sails the Black Ball Line."

FIDDLE TUNES

ANGELINE

This tune contains some echoes of Stephen Foster's "Angelina Baker,"
though the harmonic structure is different. As so often occurs in the "folk
process" one could have inspired the other.

Traditional

ARKANSAS TRAVELER

This tune was used in a medicine-show comedy routine involving a
traveling city slicker playing straight man to a banjo-picking country
bumpkin.

gCGCD   **Traditional**

149

BILL CHEATHUM

No one knows who Bill Cheathum was but the tune that bears his name
sure is a pretty one.

COAL CREEK MARCH

In his book, *The Incompleat Folksinger*, Pete Seeger relates the following: *In the 1890s black and white coal miners in Tennessee banded together to oppose the convict-labor system which threatened their livelihood. They called it the "Coal Creek Rebellion." It was marked by a series of armed skirmishes, during three years. The state militia eventually had to muster several thousand soldiers to quell the revolt. An old miner told me, "For several years the state of Tennessee couldn't collect taxes from those eastern counties."*

This is a beautiful D-tuning piece by Pete Steele of Hamilton, Ohio. It is a clawhammer adaptation of Art Rosembaum's transcription in the two-finger style.

COLORED ARISTOCRACY

Practically every old-time string band knows a version of this tune.
Watch the timing of the triplets.

THE EIGHTH OF JANUARY

This melody became a Top 40 hit in the late 1950s when Jimmy
Driftwood used it for his song, "The Battle of New Orleans." The tune
commemorates Andrew Jackson's defeat of the British at New Orleans on
January 8, 1815.

FLOWERS OF EDINBURGH

You'll have to do some finger stretching in the D7 measures, but this
beautiful tune is worth the effort.

Traditional

GASPÉ REEL

This tune comes from the Gaspé region of eastern Québec. It has achieved
a measure of recognition in Bill Spence's recording which was used as the
theme for the PBS Television show, *Crockett's Victory Garden*.

Traditional

JUNE APPLE

This arrangement is based on Wade Ward's recorded version on
Clawhammer Banjo. Uncle Wade was one of the master clawhammer
stylists.

gDGBD   **Traditional**

MISSISSIPPI SAWYER

Many pickers and fiddlers ruin a good melody by playing it too fast. Most
old-time tunes sound best at a moderate, danceable tempo.

gCGCD   **Traditional**

OLD JIMMY SUTTON

This tune has a very unusual modulation from C major in the first section
to C minor in the second. To end it, strum a C major chord at the double
bar line marked "fine."

Traditional

Fine

D.C. al Fine

OVER THE WATERFALL

This lovely melody is of Irish origin. The ending cadence, B♭ to F, gives it
an interesting modal twist. The banjo is tuned to open-C.

gCGCE

Traditional

RAKES OF MALLOW

The melody of this reel is better-known than its title. Mallow is a town in
Ireland.

Traditional

RED-HAIRED BOY

This tune is also known as "The Little Beggarman" and "There Was a
Little Soldier and He Had a Wooden Leg."

RED WING

There exists a set of ribald lyrics to this tune which can be found in the
fascinating Oak songbook entitled *Roll Me Over*, for those curious enough
to look them up or depraved enough to sing them.

ROSE TREE

In Scotland this tune is called "The Faulse Knight upon the Road"; in
Ireland, "Portlairge." A rose by any other name . . . .

SANDY RIVER BELLE

There are a number of different versions of this tune. This one, taken
from an early Bill Spence album, is my favorite.

Traditional

SOLDIER'S JOY

What "Cripple Creek" is to G tuning, "Soldier's Joy" is to double-C. Earl
Scruggs and John McEuen play a fantastic duet of this tune on the
legendary album *Will the Circle Be Unbroken* (United Artists 9801).

gCGCD   Traditional

SPEED THE PLOUGH

The title suggests the agrarian origins of this reel. It is no coincidence
that the "back to the earth" movement of recent years has been
accompanied by a rediscovery of the enjoyment of homemade music.

SWEET SIXTEEN

Yet another entry in the multiplicity of titles sweepstakes. This also goes
by the names of "Too Young to Marry" and "My Love Is but a Lassie Yet."
Art Rosenbaum mentions somewhere that he saw a rule posted in a
fiddler's club in Nebraska: "No arguing over titles of tunes." So be it.

gCGCD Traditional

THE SHAMROCK SHORE:
SONGS OF IRELAND

YOUNG RODDY McCORLEY

Roddy McCorley took part in the 1798 Rising in Toomebridge, County Antrim.

gDGBD   **Traditional**

Oh, _____ see _____ the _____ fleet - foot _____ host _____ of

men _____ who _____ speed _____ with _____ fac - es _____

wan, _____ From _____ farm - stead _____

and _____ from _____ fish - er's _____ cot _____ a -

long _____ the _____ banks _____ of _____ Bann. _____ They _____

come _____ with _____ venge - ance _____ in _____ their _____ eyes, _____ too

late, _____ too _____ late _____ are _____ they, _____ For young

Rod - dy Mc - Cor - ley _____ goes _____ to die _____ on the

bridge _____ of _____ Toome _____ to - day. _____

170

Up the narrow street he stepped, smiling proud and young;
About the hemp rope on his neck, the golden ringlets clung.
There's never a tear in his blue eyes, both glad and bright are they,
As young Roddy McCorley goes to die on the bridge of Toome today.

When he last stepped up that street, his shining pike in hand,
Behind him marched in grim array a stalwart earnest band.
For Antrim town, for Antrim town, he led them to the fray,
As young Roddy McCorley goes to die on the bridge of Toome today.

There's never a one of all your dead more bravely fell in fray,
Than he who marches to his fate on the bridge of Toome today.
True to the last, true to the last, he treads the upward way,
And young Roddy McCorley goes to die on the bridge of Toome today.

HELLO, PATSY FAGAN

This music-hall ditty presents the vainglorious stage-Irishman caricature,
so be sure to pronounce "decent" as "daycent."

gDGBD   **Traditional**

I'm work-ing____ here in Glas-gow____ and I've got a de-cent

job._____ I'm car-ry-ing bricks and mor-tar____ and me____

pay is____ fif-teen bob._____ I rise up____ in the____

morn-ing,_____ I rise up____ with the lark,_____ And____

as I'm____ walk-ing down the street you can hear the____ girls re-mark:_____

Chorus:
"Hel - lo,_____ Pat-sy Fa-gan," you can hear the____ girls all cry,_____ "Hel -

lo,_____ Pat-sy Fa-gan,____ you're the____ ap-ple____ of me eye._____ You're a

de-cent____ boy from Ire - land, that no one____ can de - ny._____ You're a

hare - um,____ scare - um, de-vil-may-care-um____ de-cent____ I-rish boy!"_____

The day that I left Ireland, 'twas many years ago,
I left me home in Antrim where the pigs and praties grow.
But since I've left old Ireland, it's always been my plan
To let the people see that I'm a decent Irishman.

Now if there's one among you who would like to marry me,
I'll take her to a little home across the Irish Sea.
I'll dress her up in satins and please her all I can,
And let her people see that I'm a decent Irishman.

KELLY, THE BOY FROM KILLANE

Written by P.J. McCall to commemorate one of the heroes of the
Rebellion of 1798.

P. J. McCall

What's the news, ____ what's the news, ____ O my bold ____ shel - ma - lier, ____ With your long - bar - rel guns ____ from the sea? ____ Say, what wind ____ from the south ____ brings a mes - sen - ger here ____ With a hymn ____ of the dawn ____ for the free? ____ Good - ly news, ____ good - ly news ____ do I bring, ____ youth of Forth, ____ Good - ly news ____ shall ye hear, ____ Bar - gey man; ____ For the boys ____ march at morn ____ from the south ____ to the north ____ Led by Kel - ly, the boy ____ from Kil - lane. ____

Tell me, who is the giant with the gold curling hair,
He who rides at the head of your band?
Seven feet is his height with some inches to spare,
And he looks like a king in command.
    O my boys, that's the pride of the bold shelmalier,
    'Mongst our greatest of heroes a man.
Fling your beavers aloft and give three ringing cheers
For John Kelly, the boy from Killane.

Enniscorthy's in flames and old Wexford is won
And the Barrow tomorrow we will cross.
On the hill o'er the town we have planted a gun
That will batter the gateway to Ross.
    All the Forth men and Bargey men will march o'er the heath
    With brave Harvey to lead in the van.
But the foremost of all in the grim gap of death
Will be Kelly, the boy from Killane.

But the gold sun of freedom grew darkened at Ross
And it set by the Slaney's red wave.
And poor Wexford stripped naked hung high on a cross
With her heart pierced by traitors and slaves.
    Glory-o, glory-o to her brave sons who died
    For the cause of long down-trodden man.
Glory-o to Mount Leinster's own darling and pride,
Dauntless Kelly, the boy from Killane.

LET ERIN REMEMBER

A song from the famous collection, *Moore's Irish Melodies*.

Thomas Moore

On Lough Neagh's banks when the fisherman strays
In the clear cool eve's declining,
He sees the round towers of other days
In the waves beneath him shining.
Thus shall memory often in dreams sublime
Catch a glimpse of the days that are over,
And, sighing, look through the waves of time
At the long-faded glories they cover.

ISN'T IT GRAND, BOYS?

There's nothing like an elegant wake to gladden an Irishman's heart,
especially when it's his own.

gDGBD   **Traditional**

Look at the cof - fin _____ with

gold - en han - dles. _____ Is - n't it

grand, _____ boys, _____ to be blood - y well

dead? _____   Chorus: Let's not have a

snif - fle, _____   let's have a

blood - y good cry. _____   And al - ways re -

mem - ber, the long - er you live, _____ the

soon - er _____ you blood - y well die! _____

Look at the flowers, all bloody withered. *etc.*

Look at the preacher, bloody nice fella.

Look at the mourners, bloody great hypocrites.

Look at the widow, bloody great female.

THE RISING OF THE MOON

Another song from the '98 Rebellion. This one by John Keegan Casey
uses the well-known melody, "The Wearing of the Green."

John Keegan Casey

Oh, then tell me, Sean O'-Far-rell, tell me why you hur-ry so? "Hush a - buch all, hush and lis-ten," and his cheeks were all a - glow. "I bear or-ders from the cap-tain, get you read-y quick and soon, For the pikes must be to-geth-er by the ris-ing of the moon."

Chorus: By the ris-ing of the moon, by the ris-ing of the moon, For the pikes must be to-geth-er by the ris-ing of the moon.

(Substitute last line of each verse in chorus as indicated in italics.)

Oh, then tell me, Sean O'Farrell where the gathering is to be?
"In the old spot by the river right well known to you and me.
One more word, for signal token, whistle up the marching tune,
With your pike upon your shoulder, by the rising of the moon."

Out of many a mud-walled cabin eyes were watching through the night,
Many a manly heart was throbbing for the coming morning light.
Murmurs ran along the valley like the banshee's lonely croon,
And a thousand pikes were flashing by the rising of the moon.

There beside the singing river that dark mass of men were seen;
Far above their shining weapons hung their own beloved green.
Death to every foe and traitor, forward strike the marching tune,
And hurrah me boys for freedom, 'tis the rising of the moon.

THE CRUISE OF THE CALIBAR

This must surely rank as one of the most tragic nautical disasters in history, comparable only to that which occurred one night on the E-ri-e Canal (q.v.).

gDGBD

Traditional

Come___ all ye dry - land___ sail - eye - ors and___
lis - ten___ to me song,_____ It's
on - ly___ for - ty___ vers - es___ and I
won't de - tain___ youse long._____ It's
all a - bout the ad - ven - ti - ures of
this poor___ Lis - burn tar _____ Who ___
sailed as man be - fore the___ mast of the
good ship___ *Cal - i - bar.* _____

The *Calibar* was a spankin' craft, pitch-bottom fore-and-aft,
Her helm it stuck out far behind, her wheel was a great big shaft.
With half a gale to fill her sail she'd do a knot per hour,
She's the fastest craft on the Laggan Canal and she's only one-horse power.

Now the captain was a strappin' man he stood just four-foot two.
His eyes were red, his nose was green, his cheeks were Prussian blue.
He wore a leather medal that he won in the Crimee War,
And the captain's wife was passenger-cook on the good ship *Calibar*.

The captain says to me, "Me lad, look here, me lad" says he,
"Would you like to be a sail-eye-or and sail the ragin' sea?
Would you like to be a sail-eye-or on foreign seas to roll?
We're under orders to Portadown with a half a ton of coal."

'Twas early the next mornin', the weather it bein' sublime,
While passin' along by the old Queen Bridge we heard the Albert chimes.
While passin' along by the gasworks straits, a very dangerous part,
We ran aground on a lump of coal that wasn't marked down on the chart.

Then all became confus-eye-on and the stormy winds did blow.
The Bo'sun slipped on an orange peel, fell into the hold below.
"Put on more speed," the captain cried, "for we are sorely pressed."
But the engineer from the bank replied, "The horse is doin' his best."

Then we all fell into the water and we all let out a roar.
There was a farmer standin' there and he threw us the end of his galluses
    and he pulled us all to shore.
No more I'll be a sail-eye-or, and sail the ragin' main,
And the next time I go to Portadown I'll go by the bloody train!

THE OLD WOMAN FROM WEXFORD

The old fella gives this tale a twist at the end. The rhythm is $\frac{6}{8}$.

gDGBD   **Traditional**

Well,   there   was   an   old   wom-an   from   Wex-ford   and   in

Wex   -   ford   she   did   dwell._____   She

lov - ed   her   old   man   dear - ly   but   an - oth - er   man   twice   as

well._____   With   me   tig - ger - y   tig - ger - y   too - rum   and   me

too - a - rum   too - a - rum   ta._____

One day she went to the doctor some medicine for to find,
Saying, "Doctor give me something that'll make me old man blind."

"Oh, feed him eggs and marrowbone and make him sup them all,
It won't be so very long after that he won't see you at all."

She fed him eggs and marrowbone and made him sup them all,
It wasn't so very long after that he couldn't see the wall.

Says he, "I'd go and drown meself but that might be a sin."
Says she, "I'll come along with you and help to shove you in."

The old woman she went back a bit to run and shove him in,
The old man blithely stepped aside and she went tumbling in.

How loudly she did yell and how loudly she did bawl.
"Yarra, hold your whist, old woman," says he, "sure I can't see you at all."

She swam and swam and swam and swam till she come to the further brim.
The old man got a fishing pole and shoved her further in.

Oh, eggs are eggs and marrowbone will make your old man blind,
But if you want to drown him you must creep up close behind.

YE HIGHLANDS AND YE LOWLANDS: SONGS OF SCOTLAND

LOCH LOMOND

In Scotland lakes are *lochs*, and Lomond is one of the most beautiful.

'Twas then that we parted in yon shady glen,
On the steep, steep sides of Ben Lomond,
Where in purple hue, the highland hills we view,
And the moon coming out in the gloaming.

The wee birdies sing and the wild flowers spring,
And in sunshine the waters are sleeping,
But the broken heart it kens nae second spring again,
Though the woeful may cease from their greeting.

COULTER'S CANDY

"Coulter's" is a favorite brand of sweets in the British Isles.

gDGBD

Traditional

Times___ are_____ get - ging hard,_____ a - roo,_____

Your__ dad - dy's sail - ing_____ on_____ the_____ blue;

Your mam - my's still_____ got a pen - ny for_____ you_____ To

buy_____ some_____ Coul - ter's_____ can — dy._____

Chorus:

Al - ly - bal - ly,_____ al - ly - bal - ly me,

Sit - ting on_____ your_____ mam - my's

knee, _____ Wait - ing for_____ your_____

wee_____ pen — ny, _____ To buy_____ some_____

Coul - ter's_____ can — dy._____

Bonny laddie, you're gettin' awful thin;
A pile o' bones covered o'er wi' skin.
Soon you'll be gettin' a wee double chin
From suckin' on your Coulter's candy.

Ah, me boy, me bonny wee man,
Run down that road as fast as you can,
Pay up your money to the sweetie-man
And buy some Coulter's candy.

MacPHERSON'S FAREWELL

The G chords in the verse are fingered so as to eliminate the B note. This
produces the harmonic effect of bagpipe drones.

gDGBD **Traditional**

Fare - well, ye dun - geons dark and

strong, Fare - well, fare - well, to thee;

Mac - Pher - son's time will no' be

long On yon - der gal - lows

tree. **Chorus:** Sae rant - ing -

ly, sae wan - ton - ly, Sae

daunt - ing - ly gaed he. He

played a tune and he danc - ed roon' Be -

low the gal - lows tree.

Take off these bands from off my hands
And give to me my sword,
For there's no' a man in all Scotland
But I'd brave him at his word.

There's some come here for to see me hung,
And some to buy my fiddle,
But before that I do part wi' her,
I'll break her through the middle.

He took his fiddle in both his hands
And he broke it o'er a stone,
Saying, "There's nae a hand shall play on thee
When I am dead and gone."

Reprieve was coming o'er the Brig o' Banff
For to set MacPherson free,
But they put the clock a quarter before
And they hanged him from the tree.

MY JOHNNY LAD

A great tune for extemporaneous versifying.

I bought a wife in Edinburgh for a bobbie And then I got a farthing back to buy tobacco wi'. And wi' you, and wi' you, and wi' you, my Johnny lad, I'll dance the buckles off my shoes wi' you, my Johnny lad.

As I was walkin' Sunday, 'twas there I saw the Queen
A-playin' at the football wi' the lads on Glasgow green.

The captain o' the other side was scorin' wi' great style;
The queen she called a policeman and had him thrown in jail.

Napoleon was an emperor, he ruled the land and sea,
He ruled all France and Germany but he didn't rule Jock McGee.

My Johnny is a bonnie lad, he is a lad o' mine,
I never had a better lad and I've had fifty-nine.

187

THE WORK OF THE WEAVERS

This was one introduced to American audiences by the Clancy Brothers
and Tommy Makem. The bouncy $\frac{6}{8}$ rhythm is tricky on the banjo but
worth the effort to master.

gDGBD   **Traditional**

We're all met to-geth - er here to sit and to
crack, With our glas - ses in our hands and our work up-on our
back. There's nay a trade a-mong 'em that can mend or can
mack If it was na' for the work o' the
weav - ers. If it was na' for the
weav - ers what would ye do? Ye
would na' have a cloth that's made of wool. Ye
would na' have a coat of the black or the blue If it
was na' for the work of the weav - ers.

There's soldiers and there's sailors and glaziers and all,
There's doctors and there's ministers and them that live by law,
And our friends in South America though them we never saw,
But we ken they wear the work o' the weavers.

The weaving's a trade that never can fail
As long as we need clothes for to keep ain other hale.
So let us all be merry o'er a pitcher of good ale
And we'll drink to the health o' the weavers.

SCOTLAND THE BRAVE

Nothing stirs a Scotsman's soul like this martial air skirled on the pipes.
It makes a fine banjo tune.

THE BANKS O' DOON

This is played in the classical style using thumb, index, middle, and ring fingers, without picks. Robert Burns turned a jaunty fiddle tune into one of his most lyrical songs.

Robert Burns

gDGBD

Ye banks and braes o' bon - ny

Doon. How can ye bloom sae

fresh and fair? How can ye

chant, ye lit - tle birds, And

I sae wea - ry, full o' care? Ye'll

break my heart, ye war - blin' birds That

wan - ton through the flow - er - y thorn. Ye

mind me o' de - part - ed joys, De -

part - ed, nev - er to re - turn.

190

Oft hae I roved by bonny Doon,
To see the rose and woodbine twine.
And ilka bird sang o' his love,
And fondly sae did I o' mine.
  Wi' lightsome heart I pu'd a rose,
  Fu' sweet upon its thorny tree.
And my false lover stole my rose,
But ah, she left the thorn wi' me.

FAREWELL TO TARWATHIE

According to Ewan McColl this was written in the early 1850s by George
Scroggie, one-time miller at Federate in the parish of New Deer,
Aberdeenshire. The same modal melody is used in the American song,
"My Horses Ain't Hungry."

gDGBD

George Scroggie

Fare - well to Tar - wath - ie, a - dieu, Mor - mond
Hill, _____ And the dear land __ of __ Crim - mond _____ I __
bid ye fare - well. _____ I'm __ bound out for __
Green - land and __ read - y _____ to sail, _____ In __
hopes to find __ rich - es _____ in __ hunt - ing the whale. _____

Adieu to my comrades, for a while we must part;
And likewise the dear lass that has here won my heart.
The cold ice of Greenland my love will not chill,
And the longer my absence more loving she'll feel.

Our ship is well rigged and she's ready to sail.
Our crew they are anxious to follow the whale,
For the icebergs do flow and the stormy winds blow,
And the land and the ocean are covered with snow.

Oh, the cold coast of Greenland is barren and bare,
No seedtime, no harvest is ever known there.
The birds here sing sweetly in mountain and dale,
But there is not a birdie to sing to the whale.

AULD LANG SYNE

In America this is certainly the best-known song of Robert Burns. The original melody is somewhat different, but this is the one we sing to welcome in the New Year.

gDGBD

Robert Burns

Should auld _____ ac - quaint - ance _____ be _____ for -

got _____ and _____ nev - er brought _____ to _____

mind? _____ Should _____ auld _____ ac -

quaint - ance _____ be for - got, _____ and _____

days _____ of auld _____ lang _____ syne? _____ For _____

auld _____ lang _____ syne, _____ my dear, _____ For _____

auld _____ lang _____ syne, _____ We'll

take _____ a cup _____ of _____ kind - ness yet _____ For _____

auld _____ lang _____ syne. _____

192

CHANTEYS AND SONGS
OF THE SEA

ROW, BULLIES, ROW

This sailor must have been a gargantuan hell-raiser to be kicked out of a wide-open town like San Francisco in 1849. Or maybe he just couldn't pay his rent.

gDGBD

Traditional

From Liv-er-pool to Fris-co a-rov-ing I went.___ To___ stay in___ that___ coun-try it was my___ in-tent.___ Bought girls and___ strong___ whis-key___ like___ oth-er damn fools,___ I soon was___ trans-port-ed back to Liv-er-pool.___

Chorus:

Sing-ing row,___ row, bul-lies, row,___ Them Liv-er-pool___ Ju-dies have got us in___ tow.___

We shipped on the *Alaska* lying out in the bay,
A-waiting for a fair wind to get under way,
The sailors all drunk and their backs is all sore,
Their whiskey's all gone and they can't get no more.

I remember one day we were crossing the line,
When I think on it now, sure we had a good time,
She was driving bows under, the sailors all wet,
She was doing twelve knots with her main skysail set.

194

And now we've arrived at the Bramleymore dock,
All the fair maids and lassies around us do flock,
Our whiskey's all gone and our six quid advance,
And I think it's high time for to get up and dance.

WHISKEY, JOHNNY

A good chanteyman could improvise rhymes to comment on immediate conditions and situations, keeping the crew in good spirits and willing to work. For his skill, and his leather lungs, he received better pay than the rest of the crew. Less-talented chanteymen simply used stock rhymes and phrases. The couplets in this chantey are typical and are interchangeable with those used in many other tunes.

Whiskey made me wear old clothes, *etc.*
Whiskey gave me a broken nose,

My dear old mother said to me,
"Son, dear son don't go to sea."

It's round Cape Horn that we must go,
Round Cape Horn in the ice and snow,

I thought I heard the first mate say,
"I treats me crew in a decent way."

I thought I heard the Old Man say,
"Tomorrow you will get your pay."

One more pull and that'll do,
For we're the boys to pull her through,

HAUL AWAY, JOE

This chantey is probably best sung unaccompanied, as all work songs are.

gDGBD   **Traditional**

Oh, when I was a little boy, some mother told me. To me! way, haul a-way, we'll haul a-way, Joe! That if I did not kiss the girls me lips would all grow mold-y, To me! way, haul a-way, We'll haul a-way, Joe!

Chorus: It's way haul a-way, we're bound for better weath-er, To me! way haul a-way, we'll haul a-way Joe!

King Louis was the king of France before the Revolution, *etc.*
Then he got his head cut off it spoiled his constitution,

Once I had a German girl she was fat and lazy,
Then I got a Yankee girl she damn near drove me crazy,

HEAVE AWAY, ME JOHNNY

With the lilt of this tune you can almost feel the deck rolling under your feet. Get some friends to harmonize on the heave aways.

gDGBD **Traditional**

There's some that's bound for New York town and some that's bound for France; Heave a - way, me John - ny! Heave a - way! There's some that's bound for the Ben - gal Bay to teach them whales to dance, Heave a - way, me John - ny boy! We're all bound to go!

The pilot he is a-waiting for the turning of the tide, *etc.*
And then, me boys, we'll be gone again with a good and a westerly wind,

Come all you hard-working sailor lads who round the Cape of Storms,
Be sure you've boots and oilskins or you'll wish you never was born,

Farewell to you, you Kingston girls, farewell St. Andrew's dock,
If ever we return again we'll make your cradles rock,

THE SLOOP JOHN B.

This is a guitarlike three-finger arrangement. The thumb plays a steady, four-beat alternating bass while the fingers pick the melody. The picking pattern in the second measure gives the basic rhythm of the piece and it would be good to memorize it before attempting the song.

gCGBD

Traditional

We come on the sloop John B., my grand-fa-ther and me, A-round Nas-sau town we did roam.

Drink-ing all night, got in-to a fight, Well I feel so break-up I want to go home.

Chorus: So hoist up the John B. sails See how the main-sail sets, Call for the cap-tain a-shore, let me go home.

home. Let me go home, I want to go home, Well I feel so break-up, I want to go home.

The first mate he got drunk, broke up the people's trunk,
Constable come aboard and take him away.
Sheriff Johnstone, please let me alone,
I feel so break-up, I want to go home.

The poor cook he got fits, throw away all the grits,
Then he took and ate up all of my corn.
Let me go home, I want to go home,
This is the worst trip I ever been on.

BLOW THE MAN DOWN

Paradise Street is in Liverpool, the most famous port in the era of the
Tall Ships. The tune will be familiar to all Popeye fans; he is frequently
heard scat-singing it just before disaster strikes.

gDGBD   Traditional

As   I   was   a- walk - ing down Par - a - dise

Street,   To   me   way,   hey,

blow   the   man   down,   A   pret - ty young maid - en   I

chanced   for   to   meet,   Give   me   some

time   to   blow   the   man   down.

She hailed with her flipper, I took her in tow, *etc.*
Yardarm to yardarm away we did go,

Aboard a Black Baller I served in my prime,
On the Black Ball Line I wasted my time,

As soon as the ship she was clear of the bar,
The mate knocked me down with the end of a spar,

From larboard to starboard we jumped to the call,
For Bully Jack Rogers commands the Black Ball,

RIO GRANDE

The Rio Grande of this song is probably a South American river, not the
one that separates Texas from Mexico. Do not use the Spanish
pronunciation for "Grande"; it has to rhyme with "sand."

gDGBD

Traditional

Oh say, were you ev - er in Ri - o

Grande? A - way

Ri - o. It's there that the

riv - er flows down gold - en sand, And we're

bound for the Ri - o Grande. Then a -

way, bul - lies, a - way, A -

way Ri - o. Sing

fare ye well me Liv - er - pool gals, And we're

bound for the Ri - o Grande.

So goodbye, fare ye well, all you ladies of town, *etc.*
We've left you enough for to buy a silk gown,

So it's pack up your duffle and get under way,
The girls we are leaving have got our half-pay,

You Liverpool Judies, we'd have you to know,
We're bound for the Horn but we don't want to go,

SANTY ANNO

General Antonio Lopez de Santa Anna was the commander of the
Mexican forces at the Battle of the Alamo in 1836.

Oh, San - ty An - no gained the day, A -
way, San - ty An - no,
San - ty An - no gained the day, All
on the plains of Mex - i - co.

Mexico, oh Mexico, *etc.*
Mexico is a place I know,

Them yellow girls I do adore,
With their shining eyes and their coal-black hair,

Why do them yellow girls love me so?
Because I don't tell them all I know,

Them Liverpool girls don't use no combs,
They comb their hair with a kipper backbone,

When I was a young man in my prime,
I kissed them Scouse girls two at a time,

The times is hard and the wages low,
It's time for us to roll and go,

THE LEAVING OF LIVERPOOL

Liverpool must be mentioned in more sea songs than any other port in
the world. This is an especially beautiful melody. Bob Dylan adapted it for
his song, "Farewell."

gDGBD   Traditional

Fare - well ___ to you ___ my ___ own ___ true -

love, ___ I am go - - ing far ___ a -

way. ___ I am ___ bound ___ for

Cal - i - for - ni - ay ___ but ___ I ___

know that ___ I'll re - turn ___ some - day. ___

Chorus:

So then fare ___ thee well ___ my ___ own ___ true - love ___ And when

I re - turn u - nit - ed we will be. ___ It's not the

leav - ing of Liv - er - pool ___ that grieves ___ me, ___ But, my

dar - ling, ___ when I think ___ of thee. ___

I have shipped on a Yankee clipper ship,
Davey Crockett is her name,
And Burgess is the captain of her
And they say that she's a floating shame.

Oh the sun is on the harbor, love,
And I wish I could remain,
For I know it will be some long time
Before I see you again.

202

RISE HER UP

The verses here are typical but the chorus is a lusty rouser. Get a crew to
harmonize on this one.

gDGBD   **Traditional**

Oh, whis - key is the life of man,

Al - ways was since the world be - gan.

Chorus:

Whis - key - o, John - ny - o,

Rise her up from down be - low.

Whis - key, whis - key, whis - key - o,

Up a - loft this yard must go, John,

Rise her up from down be - low!

Whiskey gave me stinking clothes,
Whiskey gave me a big red nose.

I thought I heard the Old Man say,
"Go ashore and draw your pay."

Me dear old mother wrote to me,
"Son, dear son come home from sea."

It's round Cape Horn that we must go
For that is where the whalefish blow.

A glass of whiskey all around
And a bottle full for the chanteyman.

THE SQUID-JIGGING GROUND

A song from the Canadian Maritimes. Squidding is one of the
messier piscatorial pursuits.

Oh, this is the place where the fisher-men gather, With oil-skins and boots and Cape Anns battened down. All sizes of figgers with squid lines and jiggers, They congregate here on the squid-jigging ground.

There's men of all ages and boys in the bargain,
There's old Billy Cave and there's young Raymond Brown.
There's a red rantin' Tory out there in a dory
A-runnin' down Squires on the squid-jigging ground.

God bless my sou'wester there's Skipper John Chaffey,
He's the best hand at squid-jigging here, I'll be bound.
Hello! What's the row? Why he's jigging one now,
The very first squid on the squid-jigging ground.

The man with the whiskers is old Jacob Steele,
He's getting well up but he's still pretty sound.
While Uncle Bob Hawkins wears six pairs of stockin's
Whenever he's out on the squid-jigging ground.

Holy smoke, what a scuffle, all hands are excited;
'Tis a wonder to me that there's nobody drowned.
There's confusion and bustle, a wonderful hustle,
They're all jigging squids on the squid-jigging ground.

Says Bobby, "The squids are on top of the water,
I just got me jigger 'bout one fathom down."
When a squid in the boat squirted right down his throat
And he's swearing like mad on the squid-jigging ground.

There's poor Uncle Billy, his whiskers are spattered
With spots of the squid juice that's flyin' around;
One poor little b'y got it right in the eye,
But they don't give a damn on the squid-jigging ground.

Now if you ever feel inclined to go squiddin',
Leave your white shirts and collars behind in the town,
And if you get cranky without your silk hanky,
You'd better steer clear of the squid-jigging ground.

WHAT DO YOU DO WITH A DRUNKEN SAILOR?

This is one of the oldest of sea chanteys. The drinking of alcohol was
strictly controlled or altogether prohibited while at sea. Once ashore,
Sailor John made up for lost time.

gDGBD   Traditional

What do you do with a drunk - en sail - or? What do you do with a

drunk - en sail - or? What do you do with a drunk - en sail - or,

Chorus:

Ear - ly in the morn - ing? Way, hey,

up she ris - es, Way, hey, up she ris - es,

Way, hey, up she ris - es, Ear - ly in the morn - ing.

Shove him in the longboat till he's sober, *etc.*

Shove him in the scuppers with a hose pipe on him,

Put him to bed with the captain's daughter,

Shave his belly with a rusty razor,

205

GREENLAND FISHERIES

Now that whales have been slaughtered to near extinction we may be
inclined to condemn the whalers of the last century and also their
whaling songs. Judging one era by the standards of another is not good
history and, in any case, these songs celebrate the adventure of old-time
whaling; they do not advocate or endorse the practice in today's world.
Sing out!

gDGBD   **Traditional**

'Twas in eight - - een hun - dred and
fif - ty - three And, of June, the
thir - teenth day, That our
gal - lant ship her an - chor
weighed And for Green - land sailed a -
way, brave boys, And for Green - land
sailed a - way.

The lookout on the crosstrees stood
With a spyglass in his hand,
"There's a whale, there's a whale, there's a whalefish," he cried,
"And she blows on every span, brave boys, *etc.*

The captain stood on the quarter-deck
And a fine old man was he,
"Overhaul, overhaul, let your davit-tackles fall,
And launch your boats for sea, brave boys,

We struck that whale and the line paid out
But she gave a flourish with her tail
And the boat capsized and four men were drowned
And we never caught that whale, brave boys,

"To lose that whale," the captain said,
"It grieves my heart full sore.
But to lose four of my gallant men,
It grieves me ten times more, brave boys,

Oh, Greenland is a dreadful place,
A land that's never green,
Where there's ice and snow and the whalefishes blow,
And daylight's seldom seen, brave boys,

SOUTH AUSTRALIA

The Land Down Under has produced some of the finest sailors in the
world.

In South Aus - tral - ia I was born, Heave a - way, haul a - way. In South Aus - tral - ia round Cape Horn, We're bound for South Aus - tral - ia. Haul a - way your rol - ling king, Heave a - way, haul a - way, Haul a - way, oh hear me sing, We're bound for South Aus - tral - ia.

As I walked out one morning fair, *etc.*
'Twas there I met Miss Nancy Blair,

I shook her up I shook her down,
I shook her all around the town,

There ain't but one thing grieves my mind,
To leave Miss Nancy Blair behind,

Oh as we wallop round Cape Horn,
You'll wish to God you'd never been born,

207

GO TO SEA NO MORE

The harsh reality of the seafaring life is, more often than not, at odds
with the romantic notions usually associated with it.

Traditional

gDGB♭D

When first____ I came____ to Liv - er -
pool____ I went____ up - on a spree.____
____ Me mon - ey____ at last____ I spent____ it
fast,____ got drunk____ as drunk____ could be,____
____ And when____ me mon - ey it was____ all
gone,____ 'twas then____ I want - ed more,____
____ But a man must be____ blind____ to____ make up his
mind____ to go____ to sea____ once more.

208

I spent the night with Angeline, too drunk to roll in bed.
My watch was new, my money too, next morning with them she fled,
And as I roamed the streets of town the whores they all would roar,
"Here comes Jack Rapp the sailorman, he must go to sea once more."

As I walked through the streets of town I met with Rapper Brown.
I asked him for to take me in and he looked me up and down,
"When I paid ye last I paid in full, with me ye chalk no score,
But I'll give you a chance and take your advance and send you to sea once more."

He shipped me aboard of a whaling ship all bound for the Arctic Sea,
Where the cold winds blow in the frost and snow, and Jamaica rum would freeze,
And worse to bear was I had no gear, for I'd lost my money ashore.
It was then I wished that I was dead, so I'd go to sea no more.

Some days we're catching whales, me boys, some days we're catching none,
With a twenty foot oar stuck in your paw we pulled the whole day long,
And when the night it came along and you dozed upon your oar,
Your back so weak you never could seek a berth at sea no more.

Come all ye bold seafaring men and listen to me song,
When you come in from those damn long trips pay mind you do no wrong,
Take my advice, don't drink strong drink, nor go sleeping with any old whore,
But get married lads and have all night in and go to sea no more.

THE MERMAID

The sea abounds with legends of strange creatures such as "fishy mermaids."

gDGBD   **Traditional**

It was Fri - day morn when we set sail,____ And we were ____ not far from the land, ____ When our cap - tain he spied ____ a mer - maid so fair ____ With a comb ____ and a glass ____ in her hand. ____

Chorus:

And the o - cean ____ waves ____ do ____ roll, ____ and the storm - y ____ winds ____ do ____ blow, ____ And ____ we ____ poor ____ sail - ors are skipping ____ at the top ____ While the land - lub - bers lie ____ down be - low,__ be - low__ be - low,__ While the land - lub - bers lie ____ down be - low.

210

Then up spoke the captain of our gallant ship,
And a fine old man was he,
"This fishy mermaid has warned me of our doom,
We shall sink to the bottom of the sea."

Then up spoke the first mate of our gallant ship,
And a fine spoken man was he,
"I have a wife in Salem by the sea,
And tonight a widow she will be."

Then up spoke the cabin boy of our gallant ship,
And a fine young lad was he,
Saying, "I have a sweetheart in Boston by the sea,
But tonight she'll be weeping for me."

Then up spoke the cook of our gallant ship
And a crazy old butcher was he,
Saying, "I care much more for my pots and my pans
Than I do for the bottom of the sea."

Then three times round spun our gallant ship,
And three times round spun she.
Three times round spun our gallant ship,
And she sank to the bottom of the sea.

ACROSS THE WESTERN OCEAN

This chantey has the same melody as "Leave Her, Johnny, Leave Her." It
is probably of Irish origin.

gDGBD   **Traditional**

Oh, the times is___ hard and the wag - es low. A -
mel - ia,___ where you bound to?___ The___ Rock - y
Moun - tains is my home. A - cross the___ West - ern
O - cean.___

That land of promise there you'll see. *etc.*
I'm bound across that western sea.

I'll make my way to Liverpool.
To Liverpool that Yankee school.

There's Liverpool Pat with his tarpaulin hat.
And Yankee John, the packet rat.

Beware those packet ships I say.
They steal your stores and clothes away.

THE HANDSOME CABIN BOY

The sailors in the fo'c's'le must have been an exceptionally unobservant
lot!

Traditional

gDGBD

'Tis of ———— a — hand — some— fe — —

male, ———— as — you ———— may— un — der - stand, ————

— Her mind ———— be - ing bent ———— on — ram — —

bling ———— un - to ———— some for - eign land, ————

— She dressed ———— her - self— in — sail - or's —

clothes, —— or so —— it does —— ap - pear, ————

— And hired ———— with ———— our— cap — —

tain ———— to— serve ———— him— for———— a — year. ————

The captain's wife, she being on board, she seemed in great joy
To see her husband had engaged such a handsome cabin boy,
And now and then she'd slip him a kiss and she would have liked to toy,
But the captain found out the secret of the handsome cabin boy.

Her cheeks were red and rosy and her hair it hung in curls.
The sailors often smiled and said he looks just like a girl,
But eating the captain's biscuits, their color did destroy,
And the waist did swell on pretty Nell, the handsome cabin boy.

'Twas in the Bay of Biscay our gallant ship did plow,
When down among the sailors was a hell of a flurrying row.
They tumbled from their hammocks, their sleep it did destoy,
And swore about the groaning of the handsome cabin boy.

"Oh doctor, dear, oh doctor," the cabin boy did cry,
"My time has come, I am undone, and I must surely die."
The doctor came a-running and smiled at the fun,
To think a sailor-lad should have a daughter or a son.

The sailors, when they heard the news, they all did stand and stare.
The child belonged to none of them, they solemnly did swear.
The captain's wife she looked at him, "My dear, I wish you joy,
For it's either you or I betrayed the handsome cabin boy."

Now sailors take your tot of rum and drink success to trade,
And likewise to the cabin boy who was neither man nor maid.
Here's hoping the wars don't rise again our sailors to destroy,
And here's hoping for a jolly lot more like the handsome cabin boy.

I'S THE B'Y

This is the unofficial national anthem of the Canadian Maritime
provinces. According to the Down-east folksinger, Gordon Bok, you can
kill a Newfoundlander by nailing his boots to the floor and playing this
song.

I's the b'y that builds the boat, _____

I's the b'y that sails _____ her, _____ I's the b'y that

catch-es the fish And takes 'em home to Li - za. _____

Chorus:

Swing your partner, Sally Thibault,
Swing your partner, Sally Brown,
Fogo, Twillingate, Morton's Harbor
All around the circle.

I took Liza to a dance
And faith, but she could travel.
And every step that she would take
Was up to her knees in gravel.

Susan White, she's out of sight,
Her petticoat wants a border.
Old Sam Oliver in the dark
He kissed her in the corner.

Salts and rinds to cover your flake,
Cake and tea for supper,
Codfish in the spring of the year,
Fried in maggoty butter.

BLOW YE WINDS

Chanteys, properly so-called, were work songs. Fo'c's'le ballads, or
"forebitters," such as this tune, were sung for amusement during slack
times. This has a fine, rousing chorus.

gDGBD   **Traditional**

'Tis ad-ver-tised in Bos-ton, New York, and Buf-fa-lo, A hun-dred heart-y sail-ors a-whal-ing for to go. Sing-ing, blow ye winds of morn-ing and blow ye winds high-o, Haul a-way your run-ning gear and blow ye winds high-o.

They tell you of the whaling ships a-running in and out;
They say you'll take five hundred sperm before you're six months out.

Now we're out to sea, me boys, the wind begins to blow;
Half the crew is sick on deck the other half below.

The skipper's on the quarter-deck a-squinting at the sails
When up aloft the lookout spots a mighty school of whales.

Clear away the boats, me boys, and after him we'll travel,
But if you get too near his flukes he'll kick you to the devil.

Now we've got him belly-up we'll tow him alongside,
Then over with the blubber hooks and rob him of his hide.

When we're back in port, me boys, and we are done with sailing,
A brimming glass around we'll pass and damn this blubber-whaling.

AMERICA'S TROUBADOR:
SONGS OF STEPHEN FOSTER

ANGELINA BAKER

No minstrel show was complete without a little ditty celebrating the charms of the singer's lady-love. She went by many names—"Ella Ree," "Lily Dale," "Lucy Long," "Melinda May," "Nancy Till," "Susan Jane." In 1850 Stephen Foster called her "Angelina Baker."

Stephen Foster

gCGBD

Oh, way down on the old plan - ta - tion, that's where I was born, I used to beat the whole cre - a - tion hoe - ing in the corn. Oh, then I work and then I sing so hap - py all the day, Till An - ge - li - na Bak - er came and stole my heart a - way.

Chorus: An - ge - li - na Bak - er, An - ge - li - na Bak - er's gone, She left me here to weep a tear and beat on the old jaw - bone.

I seen my Angelina in the springtime and the fall,
I seen her in the cornfield and I seen her at the ball.
And every time I met her she was smiling like the sun,
But now I'm left to weep a tear cause Angelina's gone.

Early in the morning of a lovely summer day
I ask for Angelina and they say she's gone away.
I don't know where to find her cause I don't know where she's gone,
She left me here to weep a tear and beat on the old jawbone.

THE CAMPTOWN RACES

This song was published in 1850 and popularized by the Christy Minstrels. It has long since become a folk standard. Soon after it came out, the sailing fraternity adapted it for the chantey, "Sacramanto" (q.v.)

Stephen Foster

Oh, the long-tailed filly and the big black horse,
Come to a mudhole and they all cut across,

MY OLD KENTUCKY HOME

Published in 1853, this song was adopted as the state song of Kentucky in 1928, and is played each year before the running of the Kentucky Derby.

gDGBD

Stephen Foster

The sun shines bright on my old Ken - tuck - y home, 'Tis sum - mer, the old folks are gay. Oh, the corn top's ripe and the mead - ow's in the bloom While the birds make mu - sic all the day. Oh, then weep no more, my la - dy, Oh, weep no more to - day. We will sing one song for my old Ken - tuck - y home, For my old Ken - tuck - y home, far a - way.

The young folks roll on the little cabin floor,
All merry, all happy and bright.
By'n by hard times come a-knocking at the door,
Then my old Kentucky home, good night.

They hunt no more for the possum and the coon,
On meadow, the hill, and the shore.
They sing no more by the glimmer of the moon,
On the bench by that old cabin door.

The day goes by like a shadow o'er the heart
With sorrow where all was delight.
The time has come when the old folks have to part,
Then my old Kentucky home, good night.

OH! SUSANNA

The first public performance of this the most popular of all Foster's
"comic" songs took place on September 11, 1847 at the Andrews Ice
Cream Saloon in Pittsburgh, Pennsylvania. Before long it was being
played and sung around the world. Along with "The Camptown Races," it
has been assumed into the oral tradition and become an American folk
song.

Stephen Foster

Well, I come from Al - a - bam - a____ with my ban - jo____ on my knee,_____ And I'm goin' to___ Lou' - si - an - a,___ my_____ true - love___ for to see._____ Oh, it rained all___ night___ the___ day___ I___ left, the weath - er___ it___ was___ dry,_____ The___ sun so hot I___ froze to death; Su - san - na,___ don't___ you___ cry._____ Oh!_____ Su - san - na._____ Oh, don't you___ cry for me,_____ For I come from___ Al - a - bam - a with my ban - jo___ on___ my___ knee._____

I had a dream the other night when everything was still,
I dreamed I saw Susanna a-coming down the hill.
The buckwheat cake was in her mouth, the tear was in her eye,
I said, "I come from Dixie Land; Susanna, don't you cry."

OLD FOLKS AT HOME

The manuscript of this song shows the name "Pedee" scratched out and replaced by "Swanee," a more euphonious choice to be sure. It was published in 1851 and rivals "Susanna" in its worldwide popularity. The tune is arranged here in the "classical" style.

Stephen Foster

Way___ down up-on the Swan - ee Riv-er,___ Far,___ far a -

way,___ There's___ where my heart is turn - ing ev - er,___

There's where the old folks stay.___ All___ up and down the

whole cre - a - tion,___ Sad - ly I roam,___

Still___ long-ing for the old plan - ta - tion,__ And for the old folks at

Chorus:

home.___ All___ the world is sad___ and drear - y,

Ev - ery - where I roam.___ Oh,___ Lord - y, how my

heart grows wea - ry,___ Far from the old folks at home.___

All round the little farm I wandered,
When I was young,
Then many happy days I squandered,
Many the songs I sung.

When will I see the bees a-humming
All round the comb?
When will I hear the banjo strumming,
Down in my good old home?

221

HARD TIMES

"Hard Times," with its melancholy lyric and hymnlike air was one of Foster's personal favorites. Recent scholarship indicates that this song was not influenced by Foster's early experience of black gospel music through his West Indian nurse, Olivia Pise. A more likely source of inspiration would seem to be Charles Dickens's novel of the same name, which came out in 1854, a year before the song. Watch the G-diminished-seventh chord on the word "weary." It's a long stretch but it makes a beautiful, weary sound.

Stephen Foster

gDGBD

Let us pause in life's pleas - ures and count its man - y

tears, While we all sup sor - row with the

poor. There's a song that will lin - ger for -

ev - er in our ears, Oh, hard times, come a - gain no

more. 'Tis the song, the

sigh of the wear - ry,

Hard times, hard times, come a - gain no more, Man - y

days have you lin - gered a - round my cab - in door, Oh,

hard times, come a - gain no more.

222

While we seek mirth and beauty and music light and gay,
There are frail forms fainting at the door.
Though their voices are silent, their pleading looks will say,
    Oh, hard times come again no more.

There's a pale, drooping maiden who toils her life away
With a worn heart whose better days are o'er.
Though her voice would be merry, it's sighing all the day,
    Oh, hard times come again no more.

It's a sigh that is wafted across the troubled wave,
It's a wail that is heard upon the shore,
It's a dirge that is murmured around the lowly grave,
    Oh, hard times come again no more.

RING, RING THE BANJO

This is one of Foster's lesser-known creations, published in 1851. It seems
an appropriate song for a banjo picker's repertoire.

Stephen Foster

The time is never dreary if a

fel-ler never moans; The ladies never

weary with the rattle of the bones. Then

come again Susanna, by the gaslight of the

moon, We'll thump the old piano when the

ban-jo's out of tune. Ring, ring the

ban-jo, I love that good old song.

Come again, my true-love, oh where you been so long?

Oh, never count the bubbles when there's water in the spring;
There's no one who has trouble when he has this song to sing.
The beauties of creation will never lose their charm
While I roam the old plantation with my truelove on my arm.

My love, I'll have to leave you while the river's running high,
But I will not deceive you, so don't you wipe your eye.
I'm going to make some money, but I'll come another day,
I'll come again, my honey, if I have to work my way.

224

JUST A SONG AT TWILIGHT:
PARLOR FAVORITES

TAKE ME OUT TO THE BALLGAME

The first World Series was played in 1903 (Boston defeated Pittsburgh,
five games to three). Five years later Albert Von Tilzer and Jack
Norworth gave our national pastime its theme song.

gDGBD

Albert Von Tilzer and Jack Norworth

THE SIDEWALKS OF NEW YORK

In 1894 James Blake was a salesman in a hatter's shop. His friend,
Charlie Lawlor, a vaudeville singer, came in one day, hummed a melody
and asked Blake to write a lyric for it. "Something about New York," said
Lawlor. The result of their collaboration became an immediate and
enduring hit. It was used as Al Smith's Presidential campaign song in
1928 and is still a singalong favorite.

gDGBD

James Blake and Charles Lawlor

East _____ Side, _____ West _____ Side, _____

All _____ a - round _____ the town, _____ The ___

tots _____ sing _____ "Ring _____ A - ros - ie," _____ "Lon - don

Bridge _____ Is _____ Fall - ing Down." _____

Boys _____ and _____ girls _____ to - geth - er, _____

Me _____ and _____ Ma - mie _____ O' - Rourke, _____

Tripped _____ the _____ light _____ fan - tas - tic _____ On _____ the

side - walks _____ of _____ New York.

227

GRANDFATHER'S CLOCK

Henry Clay Work wrote this in 1876. The notes on the twelfth fret are
most effectively played as "harmonics" to imitate the chiming of a clock.
Touch the string directly over the fret wire, but do not press it down.
When you pick the string you should hear a bell-like sound which will
continue to ring after you remove your finger from the string.

gDGBD   **Henry Clay Work**

My grand - fa - ther's clock _____ was too large _____ for the

shelf _____ So it stood _____ nine - ty years _____ on the

floor. _____ It was tall - er by

half _____ than ___ the ___ old _____ man ___ him - self, _____ Though it ___

weighed _____ not a pen - ny - weight more.

_____ It was bought _____ on the morn _____ of the

day ___ that ___ he was born, _____ And ___ was ___ al - ways his

treas - ure and pride; _____ But it

stopped   short,   nev - er to go a -

C   G   D7

gain, _____ When the old _____ man _____

G   **Chorus:**   G

died. _____ Nine - ty years _____ with - out

C   G

slum - ber - ing, _____ tick - tock, _____ tick - tock, His

              C   G

life _____ sec - onds num - ber - ing, _____ tick - tock, _____

                               D7

tick - tock, It stopped short,

G   C   G

nev - er_ to go a - gain, _____ When the old _____

D7   G

man _____ died. _____

In watching its pendulum swing to and fro,
Many hours had he spent as a boy;
And in childhood and manhood the clock seemed to know,
And to share both his grief and his joy.
For it struck twenty-four when he entered at the door,
With a blooming and beautiful bride; *etc.*

My grandfather said that of those he could hire,
Not a servant so faithful he found;
For it wasted no time and had but one desire:
At the close of each week to be wound.
And it kept in its place, not a frown upon its face,
And its hands never hung by its side,

It rang an alarm in the dead of the night,
An alarm that for years had been dumb;
And we knew that his spirit was pluming its flight,
That his hour of departure had come.
Still the clock kept the time, with a soft and muffled chime,
As we silently stood by his side,

DAISY

Written in America by Harry Dacre (nee Henry Decker), an English
songwriter, this tune was ignored by American publishers but became
immensely popular in Britain in the 1890s, even being played at the
wedding of the Duke of York. Once American audiences got to hear it
they seconded the opinion of their British cousins and "Daisy" has
remained a favorite to this day.

gDGBD

Harry Dacre

Dais - y, _____ Dais - y, _____

Give me your an - swer, do. _____

I'm _____ half _____ craz - y _____

All for the love _____ of you. _____ It

won't be a styl - ish mar-riage, _____ I

can't _____ af - ford _____ a car - riage, _____ But

you'll _____ look sweet, _____ up - on _____ the seat _____ Of a

bi - cy - cle _____ built _____ for two. _____

DARLING NELLIE GRAY

"Nellie" came out in 1856. This arrangement was inspired by Kyle Creed's
beautiful rendition on *Clawhammer Banjo*.

THE SHIP THAT NEVER RETURNED

Back in the late 1950s this old tearjerker was given a new set of words
and sold a large pile of records when the Kingston Trio sang it as "Charlie
on the M.T.A." The M.T.A. has since become the M.B.T.A. (Massachusetts
Bay Transportation Authority) but a performance of that song will still
get you a free drink in any bar in Boston.

Henry Clay Work

Well, on a sum - mer's day when the wave was

rip - pled By the soft - est, gen - tlest

breeze, Did a ship set sail with a

car - go lad - en For a port be - yond the

seas. **Chorus:** Did she ev - er re -

turn? No, she nev - er re - turned, And her

fate is still un - learned. Though for

years and years there were fond ones watch - ing, Yet the

ship, she nev - er re - turned.

There were sweet farewells, there were loving signals,
While a form was yet discerned.
Though they knew it not, 'twas a solemn parting,
For the ship, she never returned.

"Only one more trip," said the gallant seaman,
As he kissed his weeping wife,
"Only one more bag of the golden treasure,
And 'twill last us all through life.
Then I'll spend my days in my cozy cottage,
And enjoy the rest I've earned."
But alas, poor man, for he sailed commander
On the ship that never returned.

ALL THE GOOD TIMES ARE PAST AND GONE

An old Carter Family favorite. Sing it low and lonesome.

gDGBD

Traditional

All the good times are past and gone, All the good times are o'er, All the good times are past and gone, Lit - tle dar - lin' don't you weep no more.

I wish to the Lord I'd never been born
Or died when I was young.
I never would have seen your sparkling eyes
Or heard your lying tongue.

Don't you see that turtledove
That flies from pine to pine?
He's mourning for his own truelove
Just like I mourn for mine.

Don't you see that passenger train
Going around the bend?
It's taking away my own truelove
To never return again.

Come back, come back, my own truelove,
And stay a while with me.
If ever I had a friend in this world,
You've been a friend to me.

MY WILD IRISH ROSE

Since 1899 generations of would-be Irish tenors have cracked their high
notes on this old chestnut.

gDGBD

Chauncey Olcott

My wild _____ I - rish rose, _____

_ The sweet - est _ flower _____ that grows. _____

_ You may search ev - ery - where, _____ But none can com -

pare _____ With my wild _____ I - rish rose. _____

_ My wild _____ I - rish rose, _____

_ The dear - est _ flower _____ that grows, _____

_ And some - day for my sake _____ She may let me

take _____ The _ bloom from my _ wild I - rish rose.

235

GOLDEN SLIPPERS

Published by James Bland in 1879, this has long been a favorite among
old-time banjo-pickers. This arrangement is in the standard-C tuning.

gDGBD

James A. Bland

Oh, my gold - en___ slip-pers are___ laid a - way,___ 'Cause I

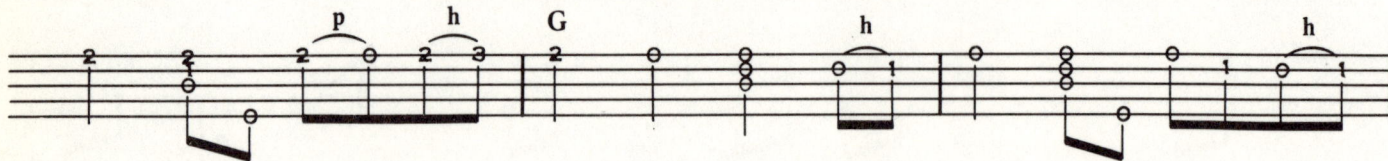

don't 'spect to wear 'em till my wed - ding day, And my long - tailed___ coat___ that I

loved so well, I will wear up in the char-iot in the morn.___

Chorus:

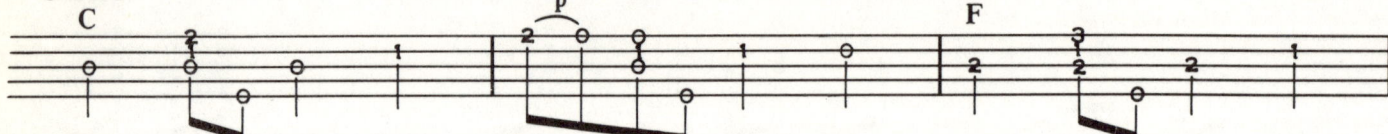

Oh,_____ them gold-en___ slip - pers, oh,_____ them

gold - en slip - pers. Gold - en slip-pers I'm___ goin' to wear Be -

cause they___ look so neat._____ Oh,_____ them

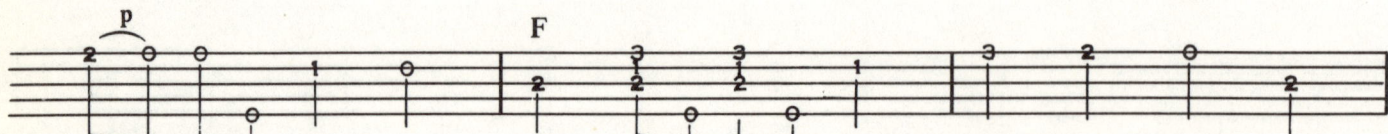

gold-en___ slip - pers, oh,_____ them gold - en slip - pers.

Gold - en slip-pers I'm___ goin' to wear To walk___ the___ gold - en street.___

And my long white robe that I bought last June,
I'm gonna get changed 'cause it fits too soon,
And the old gray horse that I used to drive,
I will hitch him to the chariot in the morn.

Oh, my old banjo hangs on the wall,
'Cause it ain't been tuned since way last fall,
But the folks all say we'll have a good time,
When we ride up in the chariot in the morn.

So, it's goodbye children I will have to go,
Where the rain don't fall and the wind don't blow,
And your woolen clothes you will not need,
When you ride up in the chariot in the morn.

CARRY ME BACK TO OLD VIRGINNY

This nostalgic ditty was published in 1878 by the famous black minstrel,
James A. Bland.

James A. Bland

gDGBD

Car - ry_____ me back_____ to old_____ Vir -
gin - ny,_____ There's_____ where the__ cot - ton__ and__ the__
corn and__ tat - ers grow,_____ There's _____ where__ the__
birds_____ war - ble__ sweet_____ in the spring - time,_____
There's ____ where the__ old_____ pin - in' heart does__ long to go.____

WHEN YOU AND I WERE YOUNG, MAGGIE

Another hardy perennial, published in 1866. The natural lilt of the banjo's rhythm will keep this sentimental favorite from becoming lugubrious.

gDGBD

George Johnson and James Butterfield

Mag - gie, _____ Since you _____ and _____ I _____ were _____

young. _____ And now_____ we are

a - ged and gray. _____ Mag - gie, _____ The

trials _____ of _____ life _____ near - ly done, _____

_____ But to me _____ you're as fair_____ as you

were, _____ Mag - gie, _____ When you _____ and _____

I _____ were_____ young. _____

FOR HE'S A JOLLY GOOD FELLOW

The air is from the French song, *"Malbrouck s'en va-t-en guerre."* A number of composers have used this theme for a set of variations. Note that the rhythm is $\frac{6}{8}$.

240

THE BAND PLAYED ON

John F. Palmer, an actor who dabbled in songwriting, wrote this at the
suggestion of his sister. After a bit of touching up by singer Charles B.
Ward, who bought the publishing rights, it became one of the biggest hits
of the late 1890s.

gDGBD

John F. Palmer

Ca - sey would waltz with a strawberry blonde, And the band played on. He'd glide 'cross the floor with the girl he a - dored, And the band played on. But his brain was so loaded it nearly exploded, The poor girl would shake with a - larm. He'd ne'er leave the girl with the strawberry curls, And the band played on.

241

IN THE GOOD OLD SUMMERTIME

In one of their best scenes, Laurel and Hardy, as street musicians, play this tune on melodeon and double bass, much to the annoyance of a workman who glares menacingly at them from the sidewalk where he is shoveling snow!

gDGBD

Ren Shields and George Evans

In the good old sum - mer - time, In the good old sum - mer - time, Stroll - ing through the shad - y lanes, With your ba - by mine. You hold her hand and she holds yours And that's a ver - y good sign That she's your toot - sie woot - sie In the good old sum - mer - time.

242

SONGS FROM TIN PAN ALLEY

BILL BAILEY

She's been pleading since 1902, but Bill Bailey still won't come home.

Hughie Cannon

gDGBD

"Won't you _____ come home, Bill Bail - ey? Won't you _____ come home?" _____ She moans _____ the whole _____ day _____ long. "I'll do _____ the cook - ing, dar - lin', I'll pay _____ the rent, _____ I know _____ I done _____ you _____ wrong. _____ Re - mem - ber _____ that rain - y eve - ning I drove _____ you out, _____ With noth - ing but a fine - tooth _____ comb? _____ I _____ know I'm _____ to blame, _____ well, _____ ain't that _____ a shame. _____ Bill Bail - ey, won't you please _____ come _____ home? _____

OUR BOYS WILL SHINE TONIGHT

The chord progression of this old tune is similar to a number of bluegrass breakdowns.

gDGBD

Traditional

Our boys _____ will shine to - night, _____

our boys _____ will shine; _____

Our boys _____ will shine to - night, _____

all down _____ the line. _____

Our boys _____ will shine to - night, _____

our _____ boys _____ will shine. _____ When the

sun goes down and the moon comes up, _____

our boys _____ will shine. _____

GIVE MY REGARDS TO BROADWAY

This is one of two hit songs from Cohan's 1904 musical, *Little Johnny Jones*.

George M. Cohan

gDGBD

Give my regards to Broadway, Remember me to Herald Square. Tell all the gang at Forty-second Street That I will soon be there. Whisper of how I'm yearning To mingle with the old-time throng. Give my regards to old Broadway, And say that I'll be there ere long.

THE YANKEE DOODLE BOY

Cohan's other hit from the show, *Little Johnny Jones*.

George M. Cohan

I'm _____ a yan - kee doo - dle dan - - dy, _____ A yan - kee doo - dle do or die, _____ A real ___ live ___ neph - ew of my Un - cle ___ Sam, _____ Born on _____ the Fourth _____ of Ju - ly. _____ I've got _____ a yan - kee doo - dle sweet - - heart, _____ She's _____ my yan - kee doo - dle joy. _____ Oh, Yan - kee Doo - dle went to _ Lon - don just to _ ride the po - nies. ___ I am _____ a yan - kee __ doo - dle boy. ___

YOU'RE A GRAND OLD FLAG

This is the big hit from the 1906 show, *George Washington, Jr.* It makes
a nice medley with the other two Cohan songs in this section.

George M. Cohan

You're a grand old flag, you're a high-fly-ing flag, And for-ev-er in peace may you wave. You're the em-blem of the land I love, The home of the free and the brave. Ev-ery heart beats true un-der red, white, and blue, Where there's nev-er a boast or brag. But should auld acquaint-ance be for-got, Keep your eye on the grand old flag.

PUT ON YOUR OLD GRAY BONNET

"I can't carry a tune, but yours kept running through my head all weekend," Percy Wenrich's publisher told him. "And any song that even I can't forget must become a hit." It did, selling over a million copies of sheet music in 1909.

gDGBD

by Stanley Murphy and Percy Wenrich

Put on your old _____ gray _____ bon - net with the

blue rib - bon on it, While I hitch _____ old _____

Dob - bin to the shay; _____ And through the

fields _____ of _____ clo - ver _____ we'll ride

up _____ to _____ Dov - er On our gold - en _____

wed - ding _____ day. _____

HELLO! MA BABY

One of the earliest hits of the ragtime era, this 1899 song capitalized on
the novelty of the recently invented "telephone."

by Joseph E. Edwards and Ida Emerson

gDGBD

G

Hel - lo! ma ba - by; hel - lo! ma hon - ey;

A7

Hel - lo! ma rag - time gal.

D7

Send me a kiss by wire,

G   D7

Ba - by, my heart's on fire.

G   E+

If you re - fuse me, Hon - ey, you'll lose me;

A7

Then you'll be left a - lone. So ba - by,

D7

tel - e - phone And tell me I'm your

G   G7   C   Cm   G

own.

BY THE LIGHT OF THE SILVERY MOON

In 1909 Henry Ford began mass-producing the Model-T, the hobble skirt was all the rage, and this song was introduced in vaudeville by the child star, Georgie Price.

gDGBD

by Edward Madden and Gus Edwards

By the light _____ of the sil - ver - y moon, _____

_____ I want to spoon; _____ to my hon - ey I'll

croon _____ love's _____ tune. _____ Hon - ey moon, _____

_____ keep a shin - ing in June; _____ Your sil - very

beams will bring love dreams. We'll be cud – dling soon, _____

_____ by the sil - ver - y moon. _____

251

PUT YOUR ARMS AROUND ME, HONEY

In 1910 Halley's comet caused considerable consternation, nearly every woman carried a parasol, and the right length for sweaters was to the knees!

by Junie McCree and Albert Von Tilzer

Put your arms a – round me hon -ey, Hold me tight.

Hud - dle up and cud - dle up with All your might.

Oh! Oh! Won't you roll those eyes,

eyes that I just i - dol - ize.

When they look at me my heart be - gins to float,

Then it starts a - rock - ing like a mo - tor - boat.

Oh! Oh! I nev - er knew an - y

girl like you.

252

HOW SWEET THE SOUND: GOSPEL SONGS

AMAZING GRACE

The text was written by the English divine, John Newton (1725-1807).
The melody is anonymous but is related to several Scottish airs dating
from the eighteenth century. Performances have ranged from an
unaccompanied solo voice to a bagpipe band. The setting here is for
traditional three-finger picking. Sing it with feeling.

John Newton

gDGBD

A - maz - ing grace, how sweet the sound That saved a wretch like me. I once was lost, but now I'm found; Was blind, but now I see.

'Twas grace that taught my heart to fear,
And grace my fears relieved.
How precious did that grace appear,
The hour I first believed.

Through many dangers, toils, and snares,
I have already come.
'Tis grace hath brought me safe thus far,
And grace will lead me home.

GIVE ME THAT OLD-TIME RELIGION

This is a "shouter" from the great tradition of black spirituals.

It was good enough for my father, *etc.*

It was good enough for my mother,

It was good for the Hebrew children,

It was good for Paul and Silas,

I AM A PILGRIM

This song is found in the repertoire of many bluegrass groups. Take it at a moderate tempo.

gDGBD   **Traditional**

I am a pil - - grim ___

___ and ___ a ___ strang - er, ___

___ A - trav - el - in' through ___

___ this wea - ri - some land, ___

___ I ___ got a home ___ in ___

___ that yon - der cit - y, ___ oh

Lord, ___ And it's not made, ___

___ not made by hand.

I got a mother, a sister and brother,
Who have gone on to that sweet land.
I'm determined to go and see them, oh Lord,
All over on that distant shore.

As I go down to that river of Jordan,
Just to bathe my weary soul,
If I could touch the hem of his garment, oh Lord,
Well, I believe it would make me whole.

256

I'LL FLY AWAY

The best gospel music communicates a spirit of joyful optimism to both
singer and audience, regardless of sectarian differences.

WILL THE CIRCLE BE UNBROKEN?

This is the best-known country gospel song of them all. It was made popular by the Carter Family, and is part of the essential bluegrass repertoire. The chorus will inspire almost any audience to join in.

I was standing by the window
On one cold and cloudy day,
When I saw the hearse come rolling
For to carry my mother away.

Lord, I told the undertaker,
"Undertaker, please drive slow,
For this body you are hauling,
Lord, I hate to see her go."

Oh, I followed close behind her,
Tried to hold up and be brave,
But I could not hide my sorrow
When they laid her in the grave.

KUM BA YAH

The title is the West Indian pidgin-English pronunciation of "come by
here." Its simple, tranquil melody has made it a favorite with Church
groups of every denomination.

Someone's praying, Lord, kum ba yah, *etc.*

Someone's singing, Lord, kum ba yah,

I CAN'T FEEL AT HOME IN THIS WORLD ANYMORE

Popularized by the Carter Family, Woody Guthrie used the melody for
one of his Dust Bowl Ballads, "I Ain't Got No Home."

gDGBD

Traditional

This world is not my home, I'm just a pass-ing through, My treas-ures and my hopes are all be-yond the blue, Where man-y Chris-tian chil-dren have gone on be-fore, And I can't feel at home in this world an-y-more.

Over in glory land there is no dying there,
The saints are shouting victory and singing everywhere.
I hear the voices calling that I have heard before,
And I can't feel at home in this world anymore.

Oh Lord, you know I have no friend like you,
If heaven's not my home, oh, Lord what would I do?
The angels take me there to heaven's open door,
And I can't feel at home in this world anymore.

JESU, JOY OF MAN'S DESIRING

As far as I know, Pete Seeger was the first to publish a banjo
arrangement of this excerpt from Bach's beautiful chorale setting. It is
taken from Cantata #147, *"Herz und Mund und Tat und Leben."*

gDGBD

Johann Sebastian Bach

LONESOME VALLEY

This is one of the best of the old revivalist hymns. Don't hesitate to make
up verses of your own: That's how a folk song evolves and grows.

gDGBD

Traditional

You got to walk that lone-some val-ley,
You got to walk it by your-self,
No-bod-y else can walk it for you,
You got to walk it by your-self.

If you cannot preach like Peter,
If you cannot pray like Paul,
You can tell the love of Jesus,
You can say he died for all.

If you want to get to heaven,
When your days on earth are through,
Just ask the Lord to show you mercy,
And shed his saving grace on you.

SINNER MAN

This is another southern revivalist hymn. It has a slightly eerie sound
from its minor modality, although the banjo is tuned to open-G.

gDGBD

Traditional

Oh, _____ sin - ner man, _____

where you___ gon - na run _____ to? _____

Oh, _____ sin - ner man, _____

where___ you___ gon - na run _____ to? _____

Oh, _____ sin - ner man.

where you___ gon - na run _____ to, _____

All _____ on _____ that _____

day? _____

Run to the rock, the rock was a-burning, *(three times)*
    All on that day.

Run to the sea, sea was a-boiling, *etc.*

Run to the Lord, Lord won't you hide me?

Oh, sinner man, you oughta been a-praying,

263

ODE TO JOY

This is the theme of the choral finale of Beethoven's Ninth Synphony. The
melody, with its scalar movement, is the essence of simplicity, but it took
a genius to write it.

Ludwig van Beethoven

SIMPLE GIFTS

The most famous of the Shaker hymns. It was written when the sect was
under the leadership of Mother Ann Lee (1736-1784). Aaron Copland used
the melody in his orchestral suite, *Appalachian Spring*.

gDGBD

Traditional

'Tis the gift_____ to be sim - ple,_ 'tis the gift_____ to be

free,_____ 'Tis the gift_____ to_____ come_____ down _____

where we ought to be, _____ And when we find_ our -

selves_____ in_ the_ place_____ just_____ right,_____ 'Twill _____

be_____ in the_ val - ley of love_____ and de - light._____

When _____ true_____ sim - pli - ci - ty is gained,_____ To

bow_____ and_ to_ bend_____ we_ will_ not_____ be a - shamed._____ To

turn,_ to_ turn,_____ will be_____ our de - light,_____ And_ by_

turn - ing,_____ turn - ing,_ we_ come_____ round_____ right._____

265

JUST A CLOSER WALK WITH THEE

In a traditional New Orleans funeral the band plays a hymn such as this
slowly and mournfully on the way to the cemetery. On the way back they
swing it out in the exuberant dixieland jazz style that leaves no listener's
spirit—or feet—unmoved.

Through the days of toil that's near,
If I fall, dear Lord, who cares?
Who with me my burden share?
None but thee, dear Lord, none but thee.

When my feeble life is o'er,
Time for me will be no more,
Guide me safely gently on,
To thy shore, dear Lord, to thy shore.

SOWING ON THE MOUNTAIN

The hallmarks of a good singalong song are: simple lyrics and a catchy
melody.

God gave Noah the rainbow sign *(three times)*
Won't be water, but the fire next time.

Where you gonna run to when the world's on fire? *etc.*
You're gonna reap just what you sow.

WAYFARING STRANGER

This song could be described as a religious ballad. It is best sung as a solo.
Gordon Lightfoot used the melody for his song, "The Way I Feel."

I'm___ just a poor _____ way - far - ing

stran - ger _____ Travel - ing through _____

___ this___ world of woe; _____ But___ there's no

sick - ness, _____ no___ toil, nor dan - ger, _____ In___ that bright

world _____ to which I go. I'm___ go - ing

there _____ to___ see my fa - ther, _____ I'm go - ing___

there _____ no___ more to roam. _____ I'm___ just a -

go - ing___ o - ver Jor - dan, _____ I'm___ just a -

go - - ing o - ver home. _____

I know dark clouds will gather round me,
I know my way is rough and steep;
But peaceful fields lie just beyond me,
Where souls redeemed their vigil keep.
    I'm going there to meet my mother,
    She said she'd meet me when I come;
I'm just a-going over Jordan,
I'm just a-going over home.

I want to wear a crown of glory
When I get home to that bright land;
I want to shout salvation's story,
In concert with that heavenly band.
    I'm going there to meet my Saviour,
    To sing His praises evermore;
I'm just a-going over Jordan,
I'm just a-going over home.

MICHAEL, ROW THE BOAT ASHORE

This song comes from the Georgia Sea Islands, a region rich in black folklore.

Mi - chael, row the boat a - shore, hal - le -
lu - - ia, Mi - chael,
row the boat a - shore, hal - le -
lu - - ia.

Sister, help to trim the sails, halleluia,
Sister, help to trim the sails, halleluia.

River Jordan is muddy and wide, halleluia,
Milk and honey on the other side, halleluia.

River Jordan is deep and cold, halleluia,
Chills the body but not the soul, halleluia.

WHEN THE SAINTS GO MARCHING IN

As any traditional jazz band will tell you, this is the most requested dixieland song of all. It's an ideal group "shout-along" for the last song of the last set, guaranteed to send an audience home humming.

Oh, when the saints _____ go _____ march - ing

in, _____ Oh,_ when the saints_____ go _____

march - ing _____ in, _____ Oh, Lord, I

want _____ to _____ be _____ in that_ num - ber _____

When the saints _____ go _____

march - ing _____ in. _____

Oh, when the revelation comes, *etc.*

Oh, when they gather round the throne,

Oh, on that hallelujah day,

JEWISH SONGS OF
CELEBRATION

SHALOM CHAVERIM

This is often sung as a round: "Goodby, friends, till we meet again."
"Shalom" also signifies "peace."

HAVA NAGILA

This beautiful, ancient melody is recognized throughout the world. It
sounds great on the banjo, played in C minor out of the G tuning.
Banjoist Carl Baron calls this "klezmer klawhammer."

gDGBD

Traditional

Hav - a _____ na - gi - la, hav - a _____ na - gi - la,

hav - a _____ na - gi - la v' _____ nis - m' - cha. _____

Ha - va ___ n' ra - n' - na, ha - va ___ n' ra - n' - na,

ha - va ___ n' ra - n' - na, ___ v' ___ nis - m' - cha. _____

U _____ - ru, _____ u - ru _____

a - chim, _____ uru a - chim b' - lev sa - me - ach,

uru a - chim b' - lev sa - me - ach, Uru a - chim ___ b' -

lev sa - me - ach, uru a - chim b' - lev sa - me - ach, Uru a - chim, ___

uru a - chim ___ b' - lev sa - me _____ ach. _____

273

CHANUKE, O CHANUKE

This Yiddish song tells the story of Chanukah, the eight-day festival
commemorating the victory of the Maccabees and the rededication of the
Temple at Jerusalem.

aDFAD

M. Rivesman

Cha - nu - kah, O Cha - nu - kah, come light the me -
Cha - nu - kah, O Cha - nu - ke, a yon - tev a

no - rah! Let's have a par - ty, we'll
shey - ner, A lus - ti - ger, a frey - li - cher, ni -

all dance the ho - rah. Gath - er round the
to noch a - zoy - ner! A - le nacht in

ta - ble, we'll give you a treat,
drey - dl shpi - in mir,

s'vi - vo - nim to play with, le - vi - vot to
Zu - dig - hey - se lat - kes e - sn

eat. And while we are
mir. Ge - shvin - der, tsindt

play - ing, The can - dles are
kin - der. Di di - nin - ke

274

burn - ing_____ low._____

lich - te - lech on._____

One_____ • for each hight,_____ they,, ___ shed_____ a sweet

Zogt_____ "Al - ha - ni - sim," loybt Got_____ for di

light_____ To re - mind_____ us of days_____ long a -

ni - sim, Un kumt_____ gi - cher tar - tn in

go._____

kon._____

One_____ for each

Zogt_____ "Al - ha -

night,_____ they _____ shed_____ a sweet light_____ To re -

ni - sim," loybt Got_____ far di ni - sim, Un

mind_____ us of days_____ long a - go.

kumt_____ gi - cher tan - -tsn in kon._____

Yehuda hot fartibn dem soyne, dem rotseyach,
Un hot in Beys-hamikdesh gezungen "Lamnatseyach,"
Di shtot Yerusholayim hot vider oyfgelebt,
Un tsu a nayem lebn hot yederer geshtrebt.

Chorus:
Deriber, dem giber,
Yehuda Makabi loybt hoych!
Zol yeder bazunder, bazingen di vunder,
Un libn dos folk zolt ir oych!

HINNEH MAH TOV

The words are from the Psalms of David: "How good and how pleasant,
that brothers live peacefully together." They should hang in the office of
every president, prime minister, and king.

eDGBD   Traditional

CHRISTMAS SONGS AND CAROLS

JINGLE BELLS

Strictly speaking this song has nothing to do with Christmas, but it
wouldn't seem like Christmas without it. Its jaunty rhythm is perfect for
the banjo.

James S. Pierpont

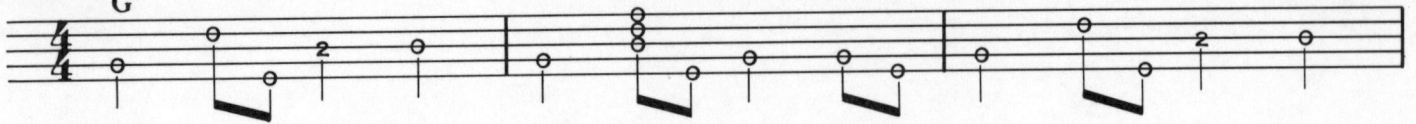

Dash - ing__ through the snow_____ in a one - horse__ o - pen

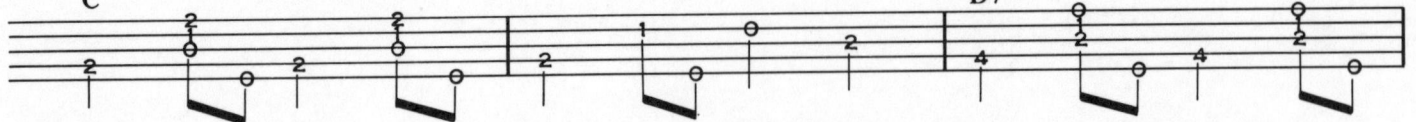

sleigh, _____ O'er the__ fields we go, _____

laugh - ing__ all the way._____ Bells on__ bob - tail ring, _____

mak - ing__ spir - its bright,_____ What__ fun it__ is to ride and sing a__

sleigh - ing song to - night._____ Oh,_____ jin - gle bells,_____

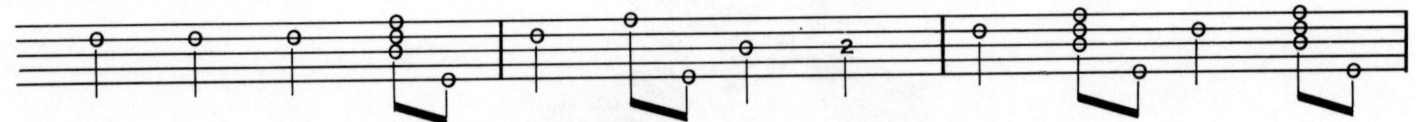

jin - gle bells,_____ jin - gle__ all the way._____

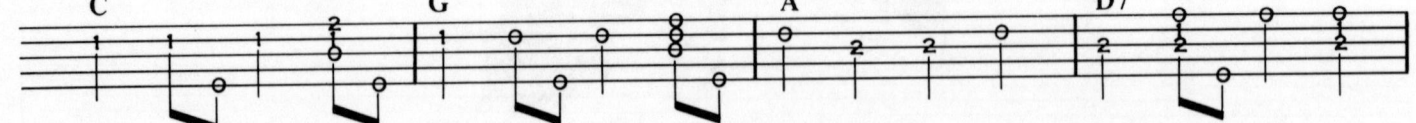

Oh, what fun it__ is to__ ride in a one - horse o - pen sleigh._____

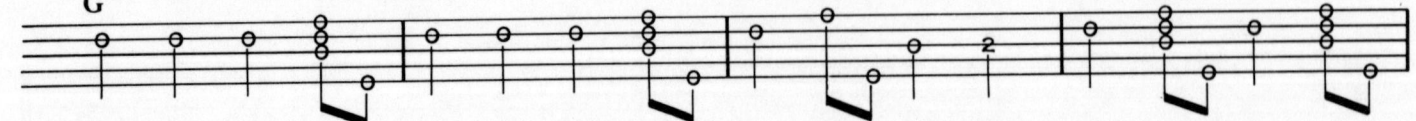

Jin - gle bells,_____ jin - gle bells,_____ jin - gle__ all the way,_____

Oh, what fun it__ is to__ ride in a one - horse__ o - pen sleigh._____

Day or two ago I thought I'd take a ride,
And soon Miss Fannie Bright was seated by my side.
The horse was lean and lank, misfortune seemed his lot,
He got into a drifted bank, and we, we got upsot!

Now the ground is white, go it while you're young!
Take the girls tonight and sing this sleighing song.
Just get a bobtailed bay, two-forty for his speed,
Then hitch him to an open sleigh and crack! you'll take the lead.

WE WISH YOU A MERRY CHRISTMAS

I love this song for the opportunity it provides annually for singing the
words "figgy pudding."

We want some figgy pudding, *(three times)*
And a cup of good cheer.

We won't go until we get some,
So bring it out here.

HARK! THE HERALD ANGELS SING

There are two other verses to this hymn, but Charles Wesley ran out of
good poetry after the first.

gDGBD

Charles Wesley and Felix Mendelssohn

Hark! the her - ald an - gels sing

Glo - ry to the new - born King;

Peace on earth and mer - cy mild,

God and sin - ners re - con - ciled. Joy - ful all ye

na - tions rise, Join the tri - umph of the skies;

With th'an - gel - ic host pro - claim Christ is born in

Beth - le - hem. Hark! the her - ald an - gels sing

Glo - ry to the new - born King.

280

GOD REST YE MERRY, GENTLEMEN

This English carol conjures up scenes of roast goose and plum pudding,
Bob Cratchit and Tiny Tim.

In Bethlehem in Jewry, this blessed babe was born,
And laid within a manger upon this blessed morn,
The which his mother, Mary, did nothing take in scorn:

From God, our heavenly Father, a blessed angel came,
And unto certain shepherds brought tidings of the same,
How that in Bethlehem was born the Son of God by name:

The shepherds, at those tidings, rejoiced much in mind,
And left their flocks a-feeding in tempest, storm and wind,
And went to Bethlehem straightway, the Son of God to find:

DECK THE HALL

This ancient Welsh carol used to be annually subjected to Walt Kelly's
Joycean linguistic assaults in his "Pogo" comic strip, emerging battered
but nonetheless recognizable as "Deck Us All with Boston Charly." The
possum was often seen strumming a banjo.

Traditional

gDGBD

Deck _____ the hall with boughs_ of _____ hol - ly, _____

Fa la la la la, _____ la la la la, _____

'Tis_____ the sea - son to_____ be_____ jol - ly, _____

Fa la la la la,_____ la la la la._____

Don we_____ now_____ our gay_____ ap - par - el.

Fa la la,_____ la la la, la_____ la la,_____

Troll _____ the an - cient yule - tide_____ ca - rol,_____

Fa la la la la,_____ la la la la._____

See the blazing yule before us, *etc.*
Strike the harp and join the chorus,
Follow me in merry measure,
While I tell of yuletide treasure,

Fast away the old year passes,
Hail the new, ye lads and lasses,
Sing we joyous all together,
Heedless of the wind and weather,

GOOD KING WENCESLAUS

In old England, St. Stephen's Day (December 26) was established as
Boxing Day. It was customary for less-fortunate people to solicit money
from patrons, employers, and others. A Christmas box was carried to
receive the gifts. Wenceslaus IV (1378-1419) was King of Bohemia and
seems to have been a pretty nice guy.

gDGBD

J. M. Neale

Good King Wen - ces - laus looked out
on the Feast of Ste - phen, When the snow lay
round a - bout, deep, and crisp, and e - ven.
Bright - ly shone the moon that night, though the frost was
cru - el, When a poor man came in sight,
gather - ing win - ter fu - el.

"Hither, page, and stand by me, if thou know'st it, telling,
Yonder peasant, who is he, where and what his dwelling?"
"Sire, he lives a good league hence, underneath the mountain,
Right against the forest fence, by St. Agnes' fountain."

"Bring me flesh, and bring me wine, bring me pine logs hither:
Thou and I will see him dine when we bear them thither."
Page and monarch, forth they went, forth they went together,
Through the rude wind's wild lament and the bitter weather.

"Sire, the night is darker now, and the wind blows stronger,
Fails my heart, I know not how; I can go no longer."
"Mark my footsteps, good my page, tread thou in them boldly:
Thou shalt find the winter's rage freeze thy blood less coldly."

In his master's steps he trod where the snow lay dinted,
Heat was in the very sod which the Saint had printed.
Therefore, Christian men, be sure, wealth or rank possessing,
Ye who now will bless the poor, shall yourselves find blessing.

SILENT NIGHT

On Christmas Eve, 1818 this hymn was first performed in the village
church of Oberndorf, Austria. A guitar was used for accompaniment
because mice had gnawed the bellows of the church organ. This
arrangement is in the guitarlike classical style.

gDGBD

Joseph Mohr and Franz Gruber

Silent night, holy night,
Shepherds quake at the sight,
Glories stream from heaven afar,
Heavenly hosts sing Alleluia;
Christ, the Savior is born!
Christ, the Savior is born!

Silent night, holy night,
Son of God, love's pure light
Radiant beams from thy holy face,
With the dawn of redeeming grace,
Jesus, Lord, at thy birth,
Jesus, Lord, at thy birth.

BIBLIOGRAPHY

BANJO

How To Play Banjo, Tim Jumper (Acorn)
Clawhammer Banjo, Miles Krassen (Oak)
Melodic Clawhammer Banjo, Ken Perlman (Oak)
Old-Time Fiddle Tunes for Banjo, John Burke (Amsco)
Old-Time Mountain Banjo, Art Rosenbaum (Oak)
Clawhammer Banjo Solos, Alec Slater (Mel Bay)
Frailing the Five-String Banjo, Muller and Koehler (Mel Bay)
The Art of the Mountain Banjo, Art Rosenbaum (Centerstream)
Banjo Styles, Larry Sandberg (Oak)

SONG COLLECTIONS

Folksinger's Wordbook. Fred and Irwin Silber (Oak)
Bluegrass Songbook, Peter Wernick (Oak)
American Favorite Ballads, Pete Seeger (Oak)
Clancy Brothers and Tommy Makem Songbook (Oak)
Folksongs and Ballads of Scotland, Ewan McColl (Oak)
Folksong Encyclopedia, Jerry Silverman (Chapell)
Old-Time Stringband Songbook, Cohen, Seeger, and Wood (Oak)
The Joan Baez Songbook (Music Sales)
The Bonnie Bunch of Roses, Milner and Kaplan (Oak)
Jewish Folksongs, Ruth Rubin (Oak)
The Ragtime Songbook, Ann Charters (Oak)
The Country Blues Songbook, Stefan Grossman, Hal Grossman, and Stephan Calt (Oak)
Folk Song U.S.A., John and Alan Lomax (Signet)

DISCOGRAPHY

ANTHOLOGIES

Mountain Banjo Songs and Tunes County 515
Clawhammer Banjo County 701
More Clawhammer Banjo County 717
Clawhammer Banjo, Vol. 3 County 757
Folk Banjo Styles Elecktra EKL-7217
Old-Time Banjo Project Elecktra EKS-7276
Southern Clawhammer Banjo Kicking Mule 213
Old-Time Banjo in America Kicking Mule 204
Melodic Clawhammer Banjo Kicking Mule 209

INDIVIDUAL ARTISTS

Art Rosenbaum: Five-String Banjo Kicking Mule 108
Art Rosenbaum: Art of the Mountain Banjo
   Kicking Mule 203
John Burke: Plain Singing and Fancy Picking
   Kicking Mule 207
Roscoe Holcomb and Wade Ward Folkways FA-2363
Uncle Dave Macon: The Dixie Dewdrop Vetco 101
Rufus Crisp Folkways FWY-2342
Dock Boggs Folkways FWY-2351
Ola Belle Reed Rounder 0021
Pete Seeger: American Favorite Ballads
   Folkways FWY-2320
Frank Proffitt Folk-Legacy FSA-1

INDEX

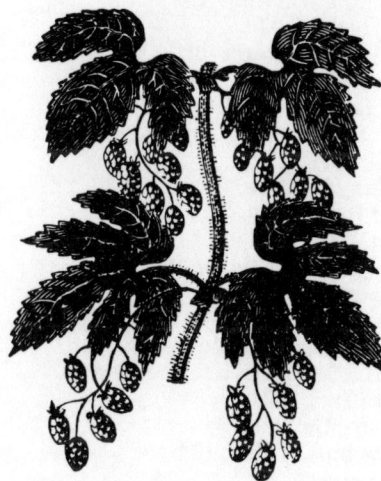

3/96(23671)